Style Me Vintage®

★

home

Photography by Heather Hobhouse

Keeley Harris

Style Me Vintage®

a practical and inspirational guide to
retro interior design

home

PAVILION

Contents

INTRODUCTION

Do you want to inject a bit of vintage style into your home, but don't know where to start?

A vintage home is something that can be easy to create – and more importantly, live with! If you want to avoid off-the-peg, flatpack living, this is the book for you.

Creating a home that functions and contains everything you need, as well as one that reflects your personality, is a difficult balance to achieve. Your home should be where your heart is; somewhere to invite your friends and family to enjoy life's milestones. Aim to make it a place to relax as well as somewhere individual with your personal touches. Opting for vintage can create a look as unique as you; not just a functional space, your home can, and should, reflect your tastes and style perfectly.

You may already own some period items of furniture or crockery, or you may never have even thought about using vintage in your home. This book aims to guide you through the styles of the different decades and, with a little extra information about key events and the designers that influenced the times, encourage you to search out special and exciting vintage finds for your home.

As a dealer in vintage ceramics and furniture for many years (I started out when I was just 15) I have gained a wealth of knowledge about the styles of previous eras, developed a keen eye for what sells and a feel for what looks good within a room setting. I enjoy the sense of satisfaction in knowing that someone loved a piece as much as I did when I bought it – giving it a revival within a different setting, instead of letting it gather dust in a corner or be thrown away.

Anyone can buy a vintage piece for their home, unlike a piece of clothing it does not have to fit you; just your home. The secret is to buy what you really love and what works for you and your space. You can mix and match eras if you want to; there are no strict rules. The key thing to remember is vintage is not just for admiring behind glass; it is functional and meant to be used.

Whether you want to style one room or the whole house, use this book to give you an insight into homes styled with pieces from the 1920s–1970s, defining how and why décor, soft furnishings and furniture differed from decade to decade. You will gain a clearer picture about each period and be able to know which key pieces to buy to get the look for your dream house.

I live in a 1960s house in Leeds and the interior has influences of 50s and 60s style, as these are the decades I most love. I don't live in a museum and enjoy mixing vintage with new items that have a vintage style – I want to encourage you to do the same. My passion is for bright colour, pattern and things that match, and this is a key theme throughout my home. I treasure my Ercol dining table, my 60s dressing table and collection of vintage ceramics. I would never part with my Taunton Vale mixing bowl and the 50s whisk I picked up years ago, even though I never bake!

The best bit about being a vintage dealer is acting as caretaker to a vast array of ceramics, glassware, artwork and lighting, looking after it as if it were my own until it leaves me to add a little bit of vintage joy to someone else's living room or kitchen. Each vintage piece has a story to tell and deserves a new lease of life.

Taking a nostalgic look back at the past offers a plethora of inspiration, giving you the tools you need to create a truly unique home. This book does not aim to help you create a 'time warp house' but instead guides you through styles, colours and items that can shape a vintage home.

The first section of this book covers vintage for the home, where to buy it and what to look for to make an impact. Learn tips about where you can go vintage hunting and arm yourself with the skills you need to be confident in buying the right things. There is a gentle brush past each decade highlighting key influences, decorative styles and must-haves. Pick up more detailed tips too as I guide you through key rooms in each decade, suggesting things to look out for and highlighting the subtle differences between some eras and the vast differences between others.

Finally, you will get a chance to look around some real vintage-styled homes – some are a pitch-perfect homage to a decade, whereas others give a nod to an era of inspiration. Find out from the owners what inspired their look. Learn about their best buys and bargains along the way, gleaning a few insider tips from them on how to create a similar look. Become au fait with recent vintage home styles that are popular and see how they draw from a variety of decades – and discover great suppliers to check out along the way.

Style Me Vintage: Home is not a price guide or an in-depth history book. This book has been written to gently guide and inspire you – to give you an 'I could do that' feeling, whether you are happy to have the odd vintage piece, mix and match the decades or decide to do a complete homage to one era. I hope that once you have read this book, you will go out and start hunting for great vintage pieces for your home. Unleash the interior designer in you and enjoy; a vintage home takes time to create, but is well worth waiting for.

WHAT IS VINTAGE?

I must say or write the word 'vintage' a hundred times or more each day, but what does this term really mean? Vintage is a word that started life describing wines and cars, but then moved into being a description used for fashion and music from previous decades. To most people it means 'high quality' or 'classic', it represents the best of its time, or something that has enduring appeal. It now describes so many things, and is often used to define a style or homage to a particular era or look.

This is where vintage for the home comes in – my take on it is that the name 'vintage' acts as an umbrella to cover six decades of design and fashionable styles. Underneath this umbrella are many very different looks that are era-specific, as well as styles and fashions that have been born out of using vintage items. For instance you might want to create a Shabby Chic, Industrial, Retro, Rustic Vintage, Eclectic or Mid-century theme in your home, and these are all of a vintage style. In this book I will introduce you to all of those era-specific looks plus the fashions, so you can then decide on the vintage look that suits you, your tastes and your home.

The popularity of vintage for the home is at an all-time high. It's ultra fashionable to reuse items and buy second-hand and turning to vintage is one way of achieving this. There is a new wave of people who may not have considered it before, joining the hordes of those die-hard vintage fans that have been buying it for years. When I tour around the UK selling at fairs and markets I am amazed at what a varied bunch my customers are; a broad range of ages and backgrounds, these people appreciate good classic design and have a genuine enthusiasm for vintage style.

Take a look online at the rapid growth of businesses selling Vintage, Mid-century and Retro, there are thousands. Look through interiors magazines and you will see plenty of references to vintage. Things that were being thrown out are now in vogue and being given a second chance to shine. Household names from the past are also re-launching heritage ranges by delving back into their archives and vintage classics are becoming influential in designs being manufactured by large modern furniture retailers too. Retro wallpaper and textiles designs are being reproduced, which is great – we are all in love with a bit of nostalgia.

Page 8: Alfred Meakin pottery in the Bamboo pattern.

Opposite: A 1930s dressing table and deco beading details on the walls sit perfectly with modern wallpaper in this guest bedroom.

The reason we want to buy vintage for the home can be ascribed to a few simple reasons:

Quality: We are now a throwaway society. The saying 'they don't make things like they used to' is quite true. In the past, pieces were made to last as homemakers expected to retain their purchases throughout their lifetime. The equivalent quality bought new today would come with a high price tag.

Value: Vintage style is easy to achieve even with the smallest budget. Be savvy and create a list of what you are looking for and how much you want to pay. Then do your research so you can get the best deal.

Recycling and Reusing: Most people today are more environmentally conscious and reusing household items will boost your green credentials. Why throw something away that is still useable?

Individuality: You can create your own style and add personal touches to a room, making a statement and putting your individual mark on a house.

Style: Vintage looks good, gives the option of creating many different looks and it can fit in within a modern home.

WHERE TO START

MAKE A CHECKLIST OF WHAT TO BUY

Taking the first steps to creating your vintage home is easier than you think. Whether you are going for a specific decade that you love or want to mix it up a bit with items that stand out, it's clear a vintage home takes some time to build. Focusing your mind on what you want to get your hands on will make the whole experience at lot more straightforward.

It's not essential to decide on a decade or vintage style instantly; this may develop when you start looking around for pieces. On the other hand, if you are already a vintage enthusiast you might have a good idea of the eras you love and the pieces you want. You might decide to build up your look by using things you have already. Often an item you fall in love with and buy on a whim will be the centrepiece that the whole room will revolve around.

Start out by compiling a wishlist for each room you want to style and highlight the items you need against those you really want.

Furniture

The style of your furniture is a key indicator of an era or vintage style – seating, display units and tables are investment pieces that set the scene. Items need to be practical, useable and durable; make sure you assess the condition of wooden furniture very carefully. Check for sturdiness, that seats are strong and that tables don't wobble. Word of warning, when looking for wooden furniture keep an eye out for woodworm!

Decorative Objects

Ornaments are the details and finishing touches that make a room. Items don't always have to have a use; they just need to look good. They are still important to pull your whole style together. Make sure that items such as mirrors, vases and ceramics are definitely on your list and do some research into what was popular for the time. Decide on the colour scheme of your room. You might work around a major object you have picked up and that dictates what you go searching for. Either way, choose colours that work well together.

Textiles

Useable in every room, textiles are easy to find and will make a big impact, giving your room the wow factor. It's probably the first thing people will comment on, so getting it right is important. Try not to use too many different patterns in one space, but use tones that complement each other. Curtains, cushions, throws, wall hangings and rugs all give that homely feeling. You can even use fabrics to re-cover and to bring a new lease of life to chairs or footstools. This is a very versatile option for your home. Make sure that textiles can be cleaned and that there are no signs of moths or deterioration that might get worse with use.

Top: A collection of original 1950s fabric off-cuts, perfect for a mid-century-styled home.

Left: Chairs come in all shapes and sizes, choose something that fits your home as well as being typical of your favourite era. Here is a 1920s bentwood chair with cane inserts.

Lighting

Practical and functional, a vintage look is completed by period lighting as it can establish the right atmosphere. Look for a range of lighting, for example, table lamps, ceiling lights and floor lamps which will provide different sources of illumination. It does not all need to be vintage, there is a good choice of vintage-style lights on the market. If you go for autentic vintage, have it checked by an electrician to make sure it is safe.

Appliances and Technology

The latest gadgets and labour-saving devices of the period bring authenticity to your look as well as something to talk about when you invite your friends around. Look out for a clock, radio, record player or kitchen appliance that was typical of the era. These may not always work, but they give a great look and dotted around the house give a nostalgic feel.

Artwork

Vintage prints and artwork can pull a room together. You don't need to spend a fortune to create a big impact with this. There were lots of iconic mass-produced poslers that can be found at fairs and markets. A low budget but effective idea is to frame vintage magazine covers and adverts depicting fashion, cars or home items of the time, which give a flavour of a certain decade. Also look out for reasonably priced sheet music, maps and education posters which highlight the artistic style of the time and provide a talking point. For framed examples to buy, check out www.vintageinprint.co.uk and www.thenostalgiashop.co.uk.

Kitchenalia

The word kitchenalia is a broad term for miscellaneous kitchen utensils, cooking and baking equipment and other items that you would typically find in kitchens. A great place to start when creating a vintage-themed kitchen, items such as jars, jugs and pots are great for the look and they can still be used. Plus items don't always have to be used in the kitchen; decorated plates can be displayed on the walls in any room, and items such as enamel can look effective in the bathroom too. There is a massive array of items that you can pick up from every era and many specialist dealers are available online and at fairs.

Storage

Including enough storage is important as we all have so many possessions and it's a good way to hide any clutter. There are lots of vintage storage solutions that can almost be a feature in the room or that can be less obvious as a place to store things. Look for the ever-popular vintage luggage, trunks, baskets, tins, wooden cupboards and sideboards as they are all great storage solutions. Style will be dependent on the era, but searching for things like this on auction sites like eBay will give you inspiration.

TOP TIP

Avoid buying too much. If you get carried away buying everything you see you will end up with a room packed to the rafters and it will start to look too cluttered. Don't forget that less is more.

WHERE TO BUY

There is nothing more satisfying for me than getting up at the crack of dawn, jumping into my van (Vera) and setting off on a buying mission. And sometimes it is a mission. Nowadays vintage style is very popular and it can be quite competitive getting hold of great finds for your home. But half the fun is the thrill of the chase!

I am always being asked 'where do you get it all from?' and the straight answer is 'a dealer never tells', well not completely anyway, as contacts and sources are hard to find. I can't give you my little black book, but what I will do is point you in the right direction and I hope you then begin to develop your own tried-and-tested ways for finding some corkers for your home.

These are my favourite hunting grounds:

Vintage and Antiques Fairs and Markets
These are a great place to start and you will find items to suit every pocket. Fairs are normally split into two types: indoors and outdoors, although some of the larger ones may have both, and there is a clear difference in the way you might find items.

Indoor fairs
These generally are set out very neatly in lines of dealers who have, in most cases, created attractive displays of their wares, nicely cleaned and neatly labelled. Some stalls might specialise in ceramics, furniture or textiles; others might have an eclectic mix of everything.

Outdoor fairs
These require more delving and digging in boxes, my favourite activity. This is where you need your hunting instincts in full working order. These kinds of dealers don't spend as much time on the way things are displayed. It may be worthwhile to rummage through what you may initially think of as rubbish to find that one interesting bargain.

Page 15: Go hunting for ceramics and crockery that are typical of the era. This a beautiful example of kitsch design by Alfred Meakin from the Circus pattern.

Opposite: Outdoor vintage fairs are treasure troves for bargain hunters.

The trick for fairs is to get there early and make sure you take plenty of cash. Most dealers don't have credit card machines and cashpoints may not be nearby. A bit of bartering is expected and if you are buying more than one item from a trader then you should always see if they will do a deal.

Remember, the dealer has to make a living, so don't overdo your opportunity to get a bargain. They will have had to buy the item themselves, clean it and transport it to the fair, so make sure everybody is happy with the deal – you may want to buy from that dealer again. Train yourself to hone in on what you are seeking as there is so much to look at, otherwise you may end up buying more than you planned.

TOP TIP

Don't hesitate – there may not be much time to decide on an item before someone else will try to snap it up under your nose. If you are certain you love it, buy it, as it may not be there if you go back for it. So many times I have had customers come back for something and it has been sold to someone else.

Auction Houses

I started going to auctions with my Dad when I was younger, so I am used to them, but they can feel a little bit intimidating if you have never been to one. Don't worry, there is not much danger of you bidding for something by coughing, but you do need to have a clear strategy and stick to it.

Make sure you arrive in good time, so that you can view the items you are interested in, most auctions have the catalogue listed online, so you can inspect what you might want to buy and make a note of the lot number. If not you can normally buy one on the day.

First job: register and get your bidding number – you will need this if you want to buy anything.

Next, examine the items you are interested in for damage and wear (some items may be listed as A/F – this means 'as found', so they could be cracked, chipped or not working) and look at general condition as well as any specific faults.

Set yourself a limit, don't get auction fever or see it as a competition you must win at all costs! If you get outbid move on, otherwise you may well overpay. This of course depends on how badly you want the item or how easy it is to find another. Keep a tally of what you have spent and bear in mind the auction house will charge fees and VAT. All your bids will need to be paid for at the end of the auction.

Take your own boxes and wrapping so you can get your items home safely. If you have bought something big, make sure you check when it needs to be collected by.

Online Auctions

Buying online through auction sites does open up a whole new world. You can search quite easily for what you are looking for, but if it's a fragile or bulky item, shipping can be challenging. The downside is you have to buy with your eyes and not your hands and you can't check the condition. There are lots of bargains to be had, particularly if you are prepared to collect the item yourself, but remember, buyer beware!

Vintage, Antique and Specialist Shops

Traditionally vintage shops were places for fashion and accessories, but now there are more specialising in vintage furniture, decorative objects and household items. Many may favour a particular style or stock items from particular eras, but they are a good place to start.

Vintage is very fashionable and many traditional antiques shops are starting to sell vintage home items more often. Don't be afraid to pop into one, they may have the one thing you seek. Antiques shops have always had furniture and interesting objects from a variety of eras, so don't discount them just because it says 'Antiques' over the door.

TOP TIP

The good thing about this kind of shop is, if they don't have something you are looking for, you can often ask if they would source a specific piece for you.

Charity and Thrift Shops

Charity and thrift shops often have specialist furniture outlets and they are a good source for furniture, mirrors and pottery. Fresh stock comes in all the time and they are always worth a quick look to see if there is something that fits the bill. Plus it's good to know that your money goes to a good cause.

Freebies

If you are the thrifty type then getting things for free is often the most thrilling. One man's trash is another's treasure, as the saying goes. I have been known to find some fantastic things that are being thrown out in a skip, given to me by a neighbour or left at the side of the road with a note on saying 'free to a good home'. Before rooting around in a skip, make sure you check with the person who has hired it, but it is amazing what people throw out. But don't just take it because it is free unless it has a practical use. You can also look on websites like Freecycle, but you might have to be quick as good vintage items tend to be snapped up quickly.

Whichever tactic you employ for sourcing vintage pieces, have fun – this is the best bit!

1920s Home

The 1920s saw the beginning of a revolution in architecture as well as the evolution of interior design in the domestic home that was set to span across the next six decades. With the 1920s vision of an ultra-modern new-age came new fashions and styles for the home.

At the beginning of the decade, the relief that the First World War had ended was expressed in revelry, it was time to party! The Roaring Twenties were born; with plenty of drinking, dancing and music at lavish cocktail parties and social occasions. Even Prohibition in the US didn't stop the fun. Jazz music flourished and socialite gals embraced new ground-breaking 'flapper' fashions.

This era saw a dramatic evolution for the home: the first interior designers created fantasy-styled rooms, encouraging bright young things to de-clutter and focus on quality not quantity. An increase in international travel meant that exotic *objets d'art* were being brought back from the Far East and Africa creating eclectic interior styles. This was also the first era of the celebrity with stars from stage and screen serving as inspiration. The classic novel *The Great Gatsby* was published in 1925 and explored the decadence of the 1920s, showing how the Jazz Age and the peak of Art Deco style made an impact. Take inspiration from the recent film for a glamorous and flamboyant 20s home.

Lifestyle magazines such as *Good Housekeeping* launched in the 20s, first in the US then in Britain, and became an instant hit. They were bought by women making homes for their Great War heroes and a lot of care and attention was spent on styling and making a home.

It is important to say that there are many blurred lines between the 20s and 30s home, and the two decades are often mentioned in the same breath. The most significant style, Art Deco, spans both eras. I plan to guide you through the subtle differences, influences and key looks that can be mixed together to create a spectacular home. Creating a 20s style gives you the chance to inject a bit of glamour and opulence into your home. It might require some investment pieces to pull it all together, but they will be worthwhile additions. If you want to create a sophisticated style for your home, choose the 1920s.

1920s Key Inspirations

- 1925 Paris Exposition
- *The Great Gatsby*
- Hollywood glamour
- Exotic travel

MAIN DESIGN INFLUENCES

There were some radical architectural design movements making a statement in the 20s that were to become the blueprint for twentieth century design and architecture from then on. Modernist design with an emphasis on form following function was the brainchild of Swiss designer Le Corbusier; his work had a massive impact on modern building styles and furniture design. His modernist aspirations certainly made their mark on history. At the same time Bauhaus, a design school in Germany, was concentrating on design and fine arts and encouraged some very influential designers of the era like Marcel Breuer.

Art Deco

'Anything goes' Art Deco is just that, a broad term coined in the 1960s used to describe a style from the 20s and 30s. The phrase was loosely used to describe every type of decoration and design in between the war years. The use of geometric and angular shapes were key features of Art Deco furniture, lighting, artwork and *objets d'art*. For a 20s Art Deco look, go for original furniture made from exotic woods such as walnut, maple and burr, but be aware these will attract top prices.

Page 21: A living room featuring Art Deco pieces of furniture and ceramics typical of the mid-20s and early 30s.

Hollywood's Golden Age

During the 20s, motion pictures inspired a highly glamorous 'Golden Age' for lifestyle and décor. Surfaces were highly polished, chrome and mirrored furniture were especially popular. Look out for opulent fabrics including velvet and silks in rich colours, with lots of black and silver too.

Exotic

Overseas travel to exotic locations influenced the newly emerging interior designers of the 20s. They created themed rooms for affluent people with the use of flamboyant and highly decorative furniture. Think black lacquered furniture with oriental scenes; birds and butterflies; Egyptian-style motifs; and black and gold colour schemes finished off with a faux zebra-skin rug.

Opposite: Sue and Ian's early 20s-inspired living room, with influences from Edwardian and Art and Crafts style, is full of family heirlooms and keepsakes. This is an achievable look, see page 30.

Designers of the 20s
- Le Corbusier – architect and furniture designer
- Eileen Gray – furniture designer
- Marcel Breuer – furniture designer

1920S DETAILS

Walls

Wallpaper was a popular choice in the 20s, although it is unlikely you would be able to find original rolls, so opt for a modern vintage-inspired example. There are lots of lovely 20s-inspired wallpapers to find. I recommend Graham & Brown who do a lovely range of Art Deco-styled ones, or Cole & Son for Art Deco or pretty floral patterns.

For a bedroom wall, look for light, delicate floral designs in pale blue, peach or lilac for a feminine tone. In somewhere like the hallway or living room go for a more dramatic Art Deco style incorporating black, silver, yellow or red motifs and patterns.

Textiles

It is tricky to find textiles from the 20s in good condition; silk was a popular material but if you find any pieces they will be quite delicate. Finding a useable example is rare and you will have to go to a specialist textile dealer.

There are other options such as embroidery on linen. Embroidery was a popular pastime in the early 20s and many ladies would create decorated textiles such as table linen and bedcovers. Any original pieces you find could be used to make cushions.

Go for heavy drapes for curtains and velvet cushions mixing vintage and new that complement your choice of wall colour. Fabrics from Liberty would suit the earlier 1920s style, but more elaborate Art Deco textiles were not mass produced until the 1930s.

Above: Original 1920s hand block-printed wallpaper. If you look closely this pattern features giraffes – portraying animals and birds on wallpapers was the height of fashion in the 20s.

Right: A page from a 1920s advertising brochure entitled *The Lure of Modern Wallpaper*, published by Lea & Son, depicting an elaborate frieze of chestnut branches.

Opposite: Embroidered 20s tablecloth and a small piece of original 20s fabric with an Egyptian sphinx pattern.

Left: This cane armchair and oriental rug work well with the exposed floorboards in this room. Interestingly the table has a removable tray top with handles, perfect for carrying in a spot of afternoon tea.

Sue and Ian's 20s-style home

"*Our style has developed organically over almost 27 years in this house. I like anything quirky or beautiful that speaks of the past, especially items that hold memories of previous generations within our family.*"

Furniture

Furniture style will depend on the particular 20s style you choose – many purist art deco homes are full of very beautiful handmade items made from exotic wood, but these can be highly priced. You can always mix old and new to get your look or go for one statement piece to work your room around.

For 20s Art Deco, look for highly polished wood cabinets, tables and chairs. Or create more of an exotic style with black lacquered cupboards, cocktail cabinets and side tables, which may also have a mother-of-pearl decoration, often displaying birds or flowers. Finally, look for bamboo and cane tables, bookcases and chairs from the 20s to create an oriental feel.

Artwork and Pictures

Try using a mixture of modern 20s-style prints, artwork and old framed photographs. Oriental and African artwork is a good thing to look out for; you can find prints in black lacquered or bamboo frames at flea markets. They may not be from the 20s, more likely to be later, but will look good all the same.

Above: Framed old photographs from the era can set the scene and show the fashions of the time too, and if they are family photos this will create a personal touch. Go for different styles of frame to give an eclectic look.

Accessories

You can finish your look off well with carefully selected accessories. Try to find Oriental rugs for a traditional look or faux zebra-skin rugs for a bit more glamour. Ornamental china vases and plates with flowers and gold details will work in any room. You will able to pick up clocks and mirrors quite easily without spending too much.

Lighting

With electricity being a recent luxury in the 1920s, lighting design was also quite luxurious; opting for an original table lamp or floor lamp will give an instant wow factor. Invest in good examples as this will be the centrepiece of your room. Chandelier-style ceiling lights will add a bit of opulence to a room and there are plenty of originals or reproductions that will give the same glamorous effect. You could push the boat out to get the art deco look with an ornate 20s table or floor lamp with globes and scantily clad women.

Top left: Original 20s rug with an Aztec pattern.

Left: Chrome and glass globe table lamp with classic Art Deco styling.

Opposite: Barbola mirrors can be picked up from antiques markets and create a beautiful period feature. Look out for prettily shaped coloured glass perfume bottles.

GET THE LOOK: 1920S

Fashionable Deco pieces of the 1920s can be difficult to find and are often budget-blowing, but they can be amazing investments! These pieces were made to the highest standards of craftsmanship, but in small quantities. Only the wealthy fashion-conscious could afford this look at the time, so only a select few adopted it – the masses kept to a simpler style. Instead, focus on the early 20s, a pre-art deco classic style which is easy to create because there is more of it available. It is an eclectic mix of that era and previous periods pulled together including the Arts and Crafts movement, Edwardian and Victorian influences. This is vintage styling at its best and there will be no shortage of items to search out. You may even have family heirlooms that can be incorporated for that personal touch.

LIVING ROOM

Make your living room both classic and comfortable with an interesting, eclectic mix of furniture and decorative items that are easy to find and quick to pull together, creating a warm and inviting space.

Key Furniture

For a 20s living room start searching for a classic sofa - a Chesterfield style with button details in leather or dark velvet is a great option. Vintage ones tend to be from a later decade, but it's the style that counts for this look.

Furniture made from wicker and bamboo was popular, you will find a variety of pieces from this period such as tables, bookcases, screens and chairs. Look out for a wicker armchair like the one in the picture on p.26. A bamboo side table will have its uses as a practical piece to put a lamp on.

A cocktail cabinet is not critical and you don't have to fill it with booze, but it's great for getting the look. It could double as storage or even a desk if it has a pull down front. They are mostly made from wood with some decorative carved detail;

Right: A cocktail cabinet and gramophone give an instant 20s look to this room. This cabinet has been converted to house a modern television.

Opposite: A Chesterfield sofa and steamer truck coffee table, which also offers great storage.

however you can find black lacquered ones which may be more expensive. Some are quite compact, so they won't take up much space. You can get a real bargain here as I have seen them go on auction sites for as little as £20.

Decorative Items

Look out for pretty vases with the typical stylised images used to decorate ceramics and fabric of the 20s. UK companies Poole Pottery and Honiton Pottery produced some fantastic colourful patterns for vases and jugs, and they are very affordable. Arrange on the mantelpiece or the top of a cocktail cabinet to finish the look.

A gramophone is the one decorative item from this period that sums up the 20s (see image on page 34). It was one of the main forms of entertainment at home and many hours of jazz music would have been played, so if you get a chance buy one, as it will give an authentic style.

If you have a fire and mantelpiece make this the focal point of the room. A dark wood over-mantle mirror, with bevelled edge glass will look great above the fireplace. Also try to find a wooden or marble 20s mantle clock, although remember you will have to wind it up every day.

TOP TIP

Old picture frames can be picked up at fairs and markets. Create atmosphere by arranging a variety of different frames, some with vintage photographs or embroidery in them. You could maybe even take a couple of elaborate ones and just frame the wallpaper. Hang them close together to create a feature wall.

Left: Reproduction version of an HMV gramophone.

Opposite top and bottom right: Glass cocktail shaker and glasses and original wooden bookends offer period details.

Opposite bottom left: Bamboo side table with decorative lace tray cloth.

Right: Classic Art Deco veneered dining set with cloud back chairs sets off this 20s dining space.

Opposite top: Honiton pottery can be picked up very easily and, although it does not all date from the 20s, offers stylised decoration.

Opposite bottom: Pictures that show the wonderful fashions of the 20s.

What To Look For: 20s Living/Dining Room

- Classic sofa - Chesterfield style with button details in leather or dark velvet
- Wicker armchair
- Oriental rug over wooden floor
- Cocktail cabinet
- Pretty embroidered cushions and soft furnishings
- Gramophone
- Ornate/floral/opulent wallpaper
- Dark wood over-mantle mirror, with bevelled edge glass
- A bamboo side table
- Dark wood mantle clock

Above: Easiwork oak kitchen unit with plenty of storage and an enamel work surface.

Left: A range cooker with tiled splashback forms the heart of this kitchen. Collect copper food moulds to hang.

What To Look For: 20s Kitchen

- Ornate china, Willow pattern
- Stoneware pots to keep utensils in
- Hang and display copper or ceramic food moulds
- A meat safe can be used for extra storage
- Oak gateleg barley twist table and Bentwood chairs
- Dark oak kitchen cupboard or dresser

Right: Tea pot and hot water jug by Royal Doulton in the Countess pattern. This has been passed down two generations and was used 'for best' in the 20s.

Below: Willow patterned plates and jugs with classic storage jars and jelly moulds form a nice arrangement.

What To Look For: 20s Bathroom

- Plant or palm on a plant stand
- Classic white bathroom suite with chrome decorative fittings or roll-top bath
- Lloyd Loom wicker chair in blue, green or pink
- Chandelier/decorative light fitting
- Dark wood towel rail
- Black and white checkerboard flooring
- Wicker laundry basket

Left: A simple but elegant bathroom with potted ferns and palms. Add a splash of 20s glamour with a pretty glass droplet chandelier.

Above and left: Pretty 20s floral wallpaper complements the feature window of this house. Look for gate-legged furniture such as this side table and again a plant finishes the look.

What To Look For: 20s Hallway

- Console table
- Plant stand
- Hall runner
- Framed sheet music to display on the stairs
- Ornate wall sconce for lighting
- Hall clock

BEDROOM

Think about creating a boudoir; with opulent textured fabrics and rich satins and silks. Find ostrich feathers and go for classic dark wood furniture. This room should make you feel like a glamorous movie star!

Dressing Table

A dressing table is an important focal point for a 1920s bedroom. The dressing table was a shrine where many hours could be spent primping and preening. Make-up was a recent innovation for women and it was important to have a comfortable location to apply it. Look for a dark wood dressing table with a round bevel edge mirror. They often have drawers either side of the mirror which are useful for storing beauty products.

Adorn your dressing table with a dressing table set in a shiny enamel or pressed glass design. Look out for ones in bright blue or green. You could finish off with a wooden jewellery box. Collect some 20s glass perfume bottles for decoration.

Accessories

Start with lighting – you don't need much, but stick to highly decorative styles. The bedside light could have a chrome or wooden base and a satin shade with tassels and fringing. The main light could be a glass chandelier with glass droplets for an opulent look.

Left: This dressing screen gives a hint of an exotic theme and the various mirrors around the bedroom help to create the 20s look.

Opposite: This bedroom has a soft feminine look with muted pink and peach tones set against the dark wood furniture.

Far right: Bedside light with tassels and fringing.

Right: A framed version of a pretty Barbola mirror that can be hung on the wall.

Look out for a dressing screen – these are very pretty, generally made of lacquered wood, bamboo or covered in a rich damask fabric. They often had birds or flowers in an oriental theme. You can also go to town with mirrors if you have space.

Look for a freestanding cheval mirror, useful for checking out your full-length profile. Barbola mirrors (moulded plaster flowers around an oval mirror) look good by the bedside or on a chest of drawers to give a definite bit of femininity. You will come across these at a flea market or vintage fair quite easily and they come in various sizes.

What To Look For: 20s Bedroom

- Dressing screen with damask fabric, or birds and flowers
- Dark wood dressing table – adorn with dressing table set
- Pretty Barbola mirror
- Ostrich feathers in an elegant vase
- Satin bedcovers decorated in floral embroidery
- Tasselled bedside light
- Wooden inlayed jewellery box
- Fan-shaped upholstered bedroom chair in peach or gold fabric
- Ornate cheval, free-standing mirror

Above: Green pressed glass dressing table set and SylvaC jug with pink ostrich feathers.

TOP TIP

Collect a variety of hand-held dressing table mirrors with pretty decorations on the back, and hang them clustered together to create a wall feature.

1930s Home

The party years of the 20s were over and there was change on the horizon on both sides of the pond moving into the 1930s. In 1929 the Wall Street Crash led to the Great Depression in America – extravagance became a thing of the past.

During the inter-war years in the UK, things were ticking along, there was a boom in house building and owning your own home was easier as mortgages became widely available. New houses of the 30s had plumbed-in kitchens and bathrooms as well as electricity, so they were becoming a lot like our homes are today.

The Depression was, however, making an impact on the home and although Art Deco style was still very fashionable, exotic woods for furniture were becoming scarce. This led to articles being made from other materials and the mass production of cheaper plywood furniture. The Deco style was still influencing more affordable textiles, clocks and electronic items such as radios and telephones.

Music was moving on from Jazz to Swing with Big Bands cheering up the nation during tough times. In the 30s many more people owned a radio and were able to listen to the likes of Glen Miller, Ella Fitzgerald and Lois Armstrong. The golden age of film prospered and the lure of the silver screen brought many people to their nearest cinema. These buildings in all their Deco splendour had opulent interiors and made a real occasion of the outing. Films such as The *Wizard of Oz* in bold technicolour gave people lighthearted relief from the looming outbreak of war.

I like the 1930s for the functional approach to design and the amazing Art Deco architecture, but also for the incredible ceramics and advertising posters of the time. I love the colour green too and many items from this period were made in that lovely 'thirties green'.

If you want to create a well-designed, functional and homely style choose the 1930s.

1930s Key Inspirations

- Modernist or Moderne style
- Deco architecture
- Aeroplanes, ships and cars
- Streamlining

MAIN DESIGN INFLUENCES

Art Deco

Art Deco was still an overriding interiors style, but in a more pared down, less flamboyant way. This was mainly because the Great Depression had a devastating effect on the luxury interiors market, people were becoming more price conscious and wanted value for money. It meant that fewer people wanted handcrafted items and they looked for mass produced products instead. Made from the latest materials, inexpensive and adaptable, they could be made to mimic the decorative surfaces typical of Art Deco in the 1920s but with a more reasonable price tag. You will discover these items are a lot easier to find, so if you want Art Deco style without breaking the bank look for mass market pieces from the 30s.

Streamline Moderne

Less ornamental, this interior style took inspiration from sleek aerodynamic principles and was quickly picked up on by car designers and architects in the 1930s. The Streamline Moderne style was responsible for those iconic white buildings featuring rounded walls, chrome fittings and horizontal lined windows.

This sleek, simple style was also adopted in the design of many everyday household objects including radios, fireplaces and furniture. Take a look at many 30s items and you will see these curved forms and long horizontal lines reproduced.

Page 45: Rachel and Dave's 1930s living room features many beautiful original vintage items from the decade. The Art Deco-style borders were done with painstaking precision to fantastic effect.

Traditional

The 1930s version of vintage style! Many people took inspiration from previous centuries as well as earlier decades: Tudor, Jacobean and Georgian styles of décor were all fashionable. These revival styles brought about a wave of reproduction furniture created in cheaper veneered woods to emulate traditional styles from previous periods. It was not high fashion, but this durable style continued into the 1940s too.

If you love the Art Deco style, but either can't afford the price tags of some earlier 1920s pieces or want to create a modernist functional space take inspiration from the 30s.

Opposite: Illustration of an elegant sitting room dating to 1931.

Designers of the 30s

- Clarice Cliff – Art Deco ceramics designer
- René Lalique – decorative glass
- Alvar Aalto – Finnish furniture designer

1930S DETAILS

Walls

Wallpaper continued to be popular, but painted walls with elaborate borders made from wooden beading achieving the angular geometric look are another option.

Wallpaper styles should be less floral; look for fan or scalloped shapes, sunbursts and chevrons.

Popular paint colours were pale green, cream and beige for living room walls. Try pale pink to add a feminine touch to the bedroom.

Textiles

New fabrics such as rayon were being used and the patterns were often quite abstract, using leaves or zigzags and chevrons in greens and oranges. Companies like Edinburgh Weavers found new ways of screen-printing fabric to incorporate these more vibrant designs. Original textiles can be found, but there are good reproductions, such as the Sanderson range, Bloomsbury Canvas.

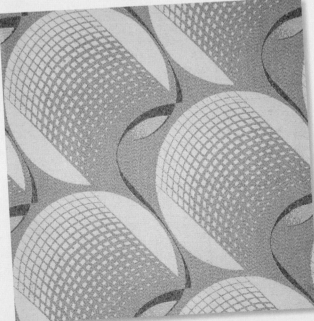

Top: A corner design from an SMB wallpaper sample book from 1934.

Left: Textile design by O.R. Plaistow. Courtaulds Ltd., 1931.

Opposite: 1930s fan-shaped mirror with bevelled glass. These look most authentic hanging from a wooden picture rail.

Flooring

Rugs were a very popular feature of a 1930s living room, giving a cosy feel to the popular wooden parquet flooring often seen in new build properties. The 1930s also saw the introduction of wall-to-wall carpets; these were in simple plain colours. Go for a plain carpet or wooden floor and then add an Art Deco style rug to get the look. Patterns tend to incorporate geometric motifs or jazz designs with zigzags of colour. See www.artdecorugs.co.uk for great wool rugs.

Furniture

It is important not to have too much furniture – less is definitely more – but think about investing in something you really love. For the living room choose a stylish three-piece suite, this could either be modern or original, but be aware that an original may well need recovering. The 30s style was for sweeping arms, preferably leather with darker piping detail.

A china display cabinet can be used in the hallway or dining room and acts as a home for ceramics. Include a dressing table in a bedroom, and add a sunburst headboard to a bed to complete the look.

Top: Abstract patterned Art Deco rug in living room with 30s armchairs and pouffe.

Right: A brightly dressed living room interior of 1937.

Opposite: Display your collection of 1930s china in a cabinet such as this original Deco version with typical arched top and glass doors.

Right: A chalkware 1930s wall plaque depicting a glamorous lady is an authentic detail in a 30s room.

Below: A bakelite telephone – these can be bought in full working order from specialist dealers.

Below right: This Arthur Woods vase is a beautiful example of affordable Art Deco style.

Accessories

Luckily 30s items were not quite as delicate as items from the 20s and were not thrown away or replaced due to the war in the 40s. You will find plenty of 30s accessories for the home. Ceramics and pottery were being produced in large volumes for the first time in the UK. Potteries like Burleigh Ware, SylvaC and Shelley were producing vases, tea sets and ornaments in bold new designs. You can pick these up at reasonable prices at auctions and on the Internet, and display in any room. Household items made in Bakelite like telephones or radios give an instant feeling of the period. Also look out for green, amber and pink-coloured glass.

Lighting

There were many options in the 30s as most homes now had electricity. Lighting was not as ornate as during the 20s, tending to be more functional in style. Opaque-coloured glass ceiling shades with a mottled effect were a common design that can be found today – they offer a pretty lighting effect. Oyster pink and soft green were popular colours. Look at fan shaped wall lights, whether vintage or modern as they reflect a soft light into the room and create atmosphere. The Anglepoise lamp was a new invention launched in the early part of the decade. This would create a more masculine statement in a living room or study. Herbert Terry is the maker's name to look out for, but more modern ones are just as good to get the look.

Left: Fan-shaped original wall light in oyster pink glass with a chrome base. These are often available as pairs.

Below left: An alabaster pendant is a perfect lighting feature if you are on a budget as they are widely available and work in any room.

Below: Classic Anglepoise lamp.

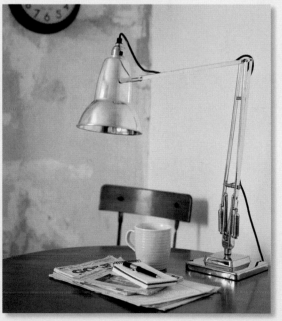

GET THE LOOK: 1930S

The 30s look is all about Deco style, but it was now more mainstream with elements of streamlining style being introduced. The look was crisper, and furniture and decoration were often simpler. Look for geometric, sleek and aerodynamic shapes. Thirties Art Deco is easier to find and therefore achievable for most of us. If you live in a 1930s house then hopefully you will have period features to work with this look, but it is just as easily achieved in any style of home.

KITCHEN

A 1930s kitchen was a light, bright and efficient space. Hygiene was important, therefore cupboards were often replaced with open shelves. These were simple in style with less decoration.

Key Furniture

If you have the room to include a vintage dresser in your modern kitchen space this will set the scene. Chrome handles on cupboard doors are a nice touch too. Get a plate rack to mount on the wall to display all of your crockery.

Look out for freestanding larder units; it was really fashionable to have one with a pull-out kitchen table cleverly designed within it to make dining in the kitchen a possibility. I have seen these for sale on auction sites and they are a very clever design solution for small spaces.

Left and opposite top: Martin and Pauline have an earlier pine dresser which has been painted and has open shelves adorned with jars, pots and enamel pieces from the 30s and 40s. They teamed this with a modern and functional kitchen.

Opposite below: This Susie Cooper Wedding Bands set is in the Kestrel shape which was influenced by Art Deco styling of the 30s.

Kitchenalia

Kitchenalia really started to take off in the 30s. Look for glass Kilner jars as they make for good storage. The best collections of stoneware pottery to start collecting from the 1930s are the T.G. Green pottery streamline pattern or blue Bretby kitchenware. Both had a range of different pots and jars you can look out for, with labels from sago to rice.

Above and right: Beautiful kitchen unit with classic sunbeam motif, chrome handles and drop-down work surface, with a collection of 30s kitchenware including T.G. Green Streamline pottery.

What To Look For: 30s Kitchen

- White dresser or kitchen cupboards with etched sunbeam motifs
- Chrome handles and detailing
- Suzy Copper, Clarice Cliff, Shelley china
- Geometric kitchen curtain fabric, with flowers or fruit motifs
- Streamline kitchen storage jars, or blue and white spotted Domino Ware – both made by T.G. Green
- Metal kitchen scales
- Bakelite pots, jugs and egg cups

LIVING ROOM

Key Furniture

Getting a three-piece suite is possible, but most 1930s ones were quite small and the elaborate Art Deco ones are few and far between. See www.cloud9artdeco.co.uk for a great selection of beautiful original versions. There are also quite a few manufacturers that create 30s-style reproduction sofas that have the rounded arms and club armchairs from this period – try www.made.com for their Jazz collection.

A china display cabinet is really easy to find, look for one with the typical geometric lines and glass doors, which often have wooden fretwork on them.

Left: Slimline china cabinet with Bakelite lamp and period pottery.

Opposite: Refurbished Art Deco living room interior. Many original features have been retained.

What To Look For: 30s Living Room

- Chrome lights or glass-etched lighting
- Stylised mirrors
- Bakelite radio
- Bakelite telephone
- Plain tiled fire surround
- Three-piece suite with rounded arms and club style armchairs
- Inlaid wood china cabinet, with sunrise shaped details
- Coloured glass bowls and vases for decoration

Accessories

Ceramics to fill your china cabinet are a must. Ceramics designers like Clarice Cliff and Susie Cooper spring to mind for classic pieces of the time. These are things we all dream of owning but would be scared of breaking. So my top tips for pottery from this period are Burleigh Ware and Alfred Meakin ceramics – less pricey than other potteries from this period, but easy to pick up, and having the colours and patterns you need to get the 1930s Art Deco look.

Opposite: Formal dining space with traditional 30s dark wood furniture, made homely with family pictures and heirlooms.

Below: Clocks are decorative as well as useful features in a room. This mantle clock shows hints of Art Deco styling but is much less elaborate than a 20s version.

Below: Pretty 1930s china. Look out for floral patterns for a softer 30s style.

60

What To Look For: 30s Bedroom

- Simple dressing table with large round or scalloped edged mirror
- Wooden wardrobe with Bakelite handles
- Enamel decorated dressing table set
- Chrome/glass-etched bedside lighting
- Plain satin eiderdown and chenille quilt
- Sunburst/fan-shaped wooden headboard
- Tub-style bedroom chair

Right: This bedroom is decorated in popular 30s green tones. Bedroom styling remained the same right into the 40s for many households and candlewick/chenille bed covers often had flower detailing, as here.

Left: A hallstand is a functional and elegant option to hang coats and hats. Often they feature storage for keys and a useful mirror to check your hat before leaving the house.

What To Look For: 30s Hallway

- Framed 30s travel prints for walls
- Oak hallstand
- Wicker baskets for storage

BATHROOM

Creating a 30s bathroom may need an element of re-tiling to get the look spot on. See opposite for a great example of tiles giving the full effect. However you don't have to go to extremes to get the look. If you have a plain white bathroom you can easy give it a quick art deco makeover. Thirties bathrooms were functional, streamlined and colour co-ordinated, and quite often pale green or white and black with an almost clinical feel.

Decorative Items

The little extras will make this look work; search for Art Deco prints of posters featuring travel or fashion and place them in plain black frames to make an immediate impact on your room. A towel rail in chrome will be a practical addition and, if you have space for a chair, choose a Lloyd Loom wicker tub chair.

An original rectangular bathroom mirror could hang over the sink; look out for ones that have a black splashback – they often incorporate a soap holder, glass holder and shelf, all with chrome fittings. If you can't find anything like this, then a traditional bevelled edge mirror on a chain will work too.

What To Look For: 30s Bathroom

- Pale green, or black and white, tiles with borders featuring geometric detail
- Chrome towel rail
- Chrome wall lights
- Rectangular mirror above the washbasin
- Framed art deco print
- Metal bathroom scales

Right: This bathroom's period details are spot on – Rachel and Dave have created a really great space. All the details tie the room together extremely well.

Opposite top: This original chrome toilet roll holder with its chevron effect is a perfect detail.

Opposite below: The green lampshade is simple but has hint of Deco styling. Both details may be difficult to find but are worth the wait.

1940s Home

Your view of home style in the 1940s will depend on where you live in the world. The Second World War was in full swing by the beginning of the 40s, sweeping across Europe. In the meantime, US home innovation was still moving forward – there were plenty of well-off households with modern appliances and newly designed furniture. In contrast, Europeans longed to have such home comforts. In the UK homes were being devastated by bombs and people were more worried about being safe in their homes than decorating and buying the latest home gadgets. However there was still a brave attempt to make do and create a homely feel.

Homemakers adopted a more thrifty style, as new items of furniture, curtains and bed linen were rationed. People turned to using hand-me-downs. Old furniture was often painted or striped to give it a lighter appearance and articles were adapted to fit into smaller living spaces. A culture of make-do-and-mend and home crafting sprang up, hand-making rugs, quilts and lampshades among other things. All of this produced a surprisingly pleasant home style that was very individual.

Home life revolved around the family, mealtimes were spent eating together, and with food being rationed Britons had to be creative with their meals. Home baking and inventing new recipes was a popular pastime. Lots of evenings were spent around the fire and listening to the radio was the favoured activity in the home.

For me, 40s style shows what can be done with tired items to bring them back to life, and it proves you don't need lots of money to create that homely vintage look. Don't be afraid to take inspiration from this decade, as there are some beautiful and practical items that can be found whilst searching flea markets and vintage fairs. Items that show signs of wear bring character to the look.

If you want to create a nostalgic, homespun, warm and cosy style for your home, choose the 1940s.

MAIN DESIGN INFLUENCES

People think that the 1940s were a drab time, but from a home interiors perspective it was not all doom and gloom. Austerity had a positive impact on furniture design – it gave some prominent designers like Gordon Russell, who was involved in the design of utility furniture, and, post-war, Ernest Race and Alvar Aalto, a chance to work with plywood and aluminium to create simplistic new furniture designs.

Eclectic

The onset of war during the 1940s meant that people did not buy new furniture and often created a look using a mix of various periods. Furniture, textiles and decorative items would be whatever you had. Creating an eclectic look is easy, it just requires you to gather up a variety of vintage items that have 'a bit of age' and work them into a fresh and nostalgic look.

Make-Do-and-Mend

This was the 'done thing' out of necessity, but the principles of doing up and making good use of items instead of throwing them away is a great principle to adopt. Taking something and re-vamping it to be used again can be a satisfying theory to embrace. Think about re-covering chairs, making cushions from curtain fabric or painting old wooden furniture. Think outside the box and search for pieces of furniture that could be used as something other than its original purpose, upcycled and transformed.

Page 69: Carrie and Michael are 1940s enthusiasts and wanted to create a warm and cosy living room, incorporating many of the items they have collected over the years.

Utility Look

In Britain rationing was in full swing and household items were being created on tight budgets with limited material available. A range of functional furniture was produced with the help of design professionals such as Gordon Russell. All the furniture and textiles that were issued at this time were marked with the CC41 stamp. Look out for this style of furniture – it's solid and simply designed and will offer an unfussy and functional look.

If you love an eclectic and nostalgic craft-inspired vintage look take inspiration from the 1940s.

Right: 1940s advertisement for Alderdale furnishing fabrics.

Designers of the 40s

- Gordon Russell – Utility furniture designer
- George Nelson – American Modernist furniture designer
- Christian Dior – fashion

1940S DETAILS

Walls

Walls should be of muted tones or pastel colours; subtle wallpaper defines the style, and floral papers with natural rose patterns can work within most rooms. You could always go for warm cream-painted walls or wood panelling half way up a wall to allow for soft furnishings that are patterned.

Textiles

The right textiles give that warm and homespun feel to this look, so spend time finding the right pieces. Look for pretty floral fabrics – you should have plenty to choose from. Wool blankets are a good buy as well as odd bits of mix and match fabric. Knitting and crochet was popular; and all manner of throws and cushions can be put on sofas or chairs.

Original patchwork quilts can be used to cover beds, or if they're not in such good condition use them to make cushions. Eiderdowns filled with duck feathers were originally used on top of blankets for warmth, but for a more modern twist use one across the bottom of the bed as a decorative feature against a plain cover.

Top: An original piece of 40s fabric, which was found still wrapped in brown paper from the drapers. New fabric was rationed during the war and people had to reuse fabric to make items for the home.

Left: A selection of eiderdowns in pretty floral fabrics.

Left: This pretty 40s-inspired bedroom features a contrast of textiles with florals and patchwork.

Above: An example of the CC41 stamp that can be found on furniture made during wartime rationing in Britain. This utility furniture was simple in design and functional and available to newlyweds and those who had been bombed during the war.

Left: Stacks of suitcases give a nostalgic 40s feeling to a room but are also useful as tables and storage.

Furniture

Furniture can be mismatched, painted or made out of other things. Consider what different items could be used for and what you need within your space. A wooden bookcase or tallboy in the simple utility style would be useful. Collect up old suitcases which can be used as handy storage. Look for items that are worn and well-used – leather items and painted furniture can give this feel.

Above: Old office drawers or collector's cabinets can be reused around the house for paperwork and general bits and bobs. The odd scratch or scuff adds character.

Left: Why not look out for an original rag rug? The one in this picture was passed down through the family.

Artwork and Pictures

Think creatively about what could be used to hang on your walls that is not just a standard picture in a frame. Have fun collecting interesting items from flea markets and vintage fairs to offer a bit of nostalgia. Use old black and white photographs, whether they are of family or buildings, they offer a taste of social history. Enamel adverts and signs from the period can be hung in the kitchen or bathroom.

Frame postcards with pretty illustrations and flick through old magazines for images to use. Collect old sheet music, many new songs were written in the 40s and people would enjoy a sing-song around the piano – the front covers often have wonderfully nostalgic illustrations.

Opposite: A selection of framed 40s items including an embroidery sample, sheet music, and a biscuit advert.

Below: Enamel railway signs as well as advertising signs make a talking point and create an interesting wall feature.

Below: Rags have been used here to create a piece of art. As the name suggests, rag rugs are made from strips of material, often cut from old clothes or blankets – a great way to 'make do and mend'.

Accessories

You can finish off your 40s look room with carefully selected accessories that would have been around at the time. Look for pretty floral cups and saucers, and plates in pastel colours for decoration.

Old packaging and advertising will look great in the kitchen as well as a wartime radio. Adorn shelves with old books, photo frames and pretty glass vases.

Lighting

Lighting design had not really moved on much from the styles of the 30s, so some of the less decorative glass shades from this period would suit this look. Standard lamps with a floral shade are great for the living room. People often made their own lampshades with leftover fabric and this is something you too can try, maybe incorporating old buttons too.

Top: A collection of advertising jars and packaging – these are quite hard to track down but the designs are amazing.

Left: On the mantelpiece, a selection of old family photos and period vase.

Opposite: Having a radio from the 1940s, in working order or not, is a great nod to how important they were to keep everyone up to date with current affairs of the time.

GET THE LOOK: 1940S

There was not a great deal of development in interior design during the early 1940s in Britain; lots of décor and furnishings stayed the same as in the previous two decades. With very few references to a particular 40s style being available, embrace the idea of a homespun, warm and nostalgic style. 'Make-do-and-mend' was a wartime slogan, but if you employ this principle for a 1940s look you will create something far from drab.

KITCHEN

The 1940s kitchen was the hub of the household and the whole family would spend lots of time around the kitchen table, as it was warm and there was home-cooked food. Home cooking was extremely important and although the fitted kitchen had not arrived just yet, the kitchen was perfectly formed and well-equipped with lots of baking paraphernalia, pots and pans.

Furniture

A pine dresser is a great place to start when looking for kitchen furniture, it will allow you to display plates and crockery, and the drawers and cupboards offer a place for utensils and glasswear. If it has a slightly distressed look then so much the better.

Look for a solid pine table too if your kitchen allows space for one. You can also use mismatched chairs of different styles and colours for a great make-do-and-mend style.

Above: Collect up a nice selection of original kitchenware.

Opposite: Enamel bread bins, pots and pans are ideal – don't be put off by dents and rust, they are just showing their age!

BREAD

Above: A selection of Beryl Ware in green. It's also available in pink, blue and pale yellow – try mixing and matching the colours.

What to Look For: 40s Kitchen

- Pine dresser to display crockery and jars
- Large pine table and mismatched wooden chairs to add character
- Plain pastel coloured Beryl Ware by Woods Pottery
- Enamel breadbin and cooking pots
- Jelly moulds
- Tins
- Butter dish
- Wicker shopping baskets
- Old wooden delivery crates

Kitchenalia

Look for any pottery from the era, or tins, jars, dishes and plates. Wood & Sons' 'Beryl Ware' was a range of utility crockery without fancy decoration – it came in pastel pink, blue, yellow and green. Very hard-wearing, it is perfect for everyday use. If you mix up the colours it will look great on the dresser and go with the tones of other items from this period.

Enamelware such as breadbins, jugs, pots and pans are very authentic, mainly in white and blue or cream and green, they are very useable kitchen items. Look out for teapots and kettles with the Judge label on the lid as these are definitely from the 1940s, but other slightly newer European versions look just as good.

Above: 1940s Mintons storage jars - the Art Deco streamline effect continued from the 30s.

Opposite: A pretty floral mirror for the bathroom. Foxing (when the silver backing has deteriorated) is just a sign of age.

What to Look For: 40s Bathroom

- White tiles and suite
- Towel rail
- Wicker laundry basket
- Ceramic soap dish
- Pale pink accessories and textiles
- China cabinet or tea trolley to store towels
- Large Barbola mirror or cream wooden mirror
- Enamel pots and jugs for decoration

Carrie and Michael's 40s-style home

"We like the 1940s and are interested in vintage cars and WW2, as well as enjoying big band music from the era. We wanted to create a warm and cosy house full of nostalgia."

Top Tip

Group collections together on shelves to create a feature in a room. We have done this in our sun room. This way we can enjoy looking at the items whenever we want instead of them being locked away in a cabinet.

TOP TIP

Tea trolleys were used a lot in the 40s in tearooms and at home. Find a new or used one for your bathroom as a handy place for towels and toiletries.

LIVING ROOM

Most 1940s living rooms looked much like 1930s ones, but they were becoming tired and worn. The only way to bring a bit of life to tired armchairs was to re-cover them with remnants of material or old bedding. Re-using things and making them into something else is a great concept to employ when creating a wartime chic living room. The results can be surprisingly stylish, all it takes is a bit of imagination.

Furniture

Look for a pair of worn leather armchairs to give that lived-in look. An oak writing bureau is perfect for storage and can even house a modern laptop. Barley twist side tables are easy to find and can be left in original condition or painted.

Collect up vintage luggage, they create perfect storage in a living room and look great. Another option is to get a steamer trunk. These are more durable and have a harder case, making the perfect coffee table – you can store your magazines and books inside too.

Finishing Touches

Make cushions using vintage headscarves – often silk and with pretty florals they make really nice soft furnishings. Ragrugs were a very popular thing to make in the war years. You can use the same technique and make an interesting rug from old scraps of material or look around for an original at a vintage market.

Finish off the wartime feeling with a radio and some cosy crocheted blankets, and you will have a very homely, cosy feel to your living space.

What to Look For: 40s Living Room

- Worn leather armchairs
- Embroidered linen or crocheted cushions
- Rag rugs
- Wooden or Bakelite radio
- Steamer trunk with wooden banding
- Granny square crochet blanket
- Oak bookcase or bureaux
- Barley twist side table
- Embroidered fire screen

Left: An embroidered fire screen.

Opposite: A comfy armchair by the fire gives a cosy feeling to a room.

What to Look For: 40s Bedroom

- Oak tallboy cupboard
- Stack brown leather suitcases for storage
- Patchwork quilts of floral fabrics
- Flower pictures and framed embroidery
- Lloyd Loom chair
- Wooden blanket box
- Metal framed bed
- Decorative hatboxes

TOP TIP

Stack hatboxes and suitcases on top of a wardrobe, they look great and offer additional storage.

Top: Look out for SylvaC ceramic animals, which often came in green or fawn. This little fella is happy on the dressing table with other keepsakes.

Left: 1940s baskets are often very decorative with pretty flowers woven on the side. They are a good place to store trinkets.

Pauline and Martin's 40s-style home

" *For us it's all about the textiles from this era and earlier, so our style is pretty curtains, quilts, eiderdowns and beautiful upholstered chairs.* "

Right: If you have a collection of vintage clothes and hats why not display them, rather than keeping them closed up in a wardrobe?

1950s Home

The 1950s were a bright and optimistic time; there was a new sense of extravagance in households who were not restrained by the austerity of the war years – and this led to a boom in home decorating. Creating a 50s feel in your home means you can choose from a variety of styles, abstract patterns and colours. Smart and functional or kitsch and fun, the 50s waved goodbye to the drab and introduced homeowners to the future with a bang.

In the UK in 1951, the Festival of Britain took place offering visitors a glimpse into the future of design and innovation. It opened up a whole new world of contemporary design; influenced by a wave of new designers that came through towards the end of the 40s. Their flowing designs took advantage of new materials and manufacturing techniques.

Art and design took inspiration from the nuclear age as well as the Soviet Union's launch of the first satellite in space: Sputnik. Many textiles and lighting designs of the 50s incorporated atomic-style shapes, these are what make the 50s style so unique.

Rock 'n' roll was the big new music trend to come over from America and teenagers hung out in coffee bars playing music on the jukebox. This was also the era of television; it became the new focal point of the room, and TV advertising also started to influence what people wanted to buy. Newlyweds had more flexible options to furnish and decorate their homes with the introduction of hire purchase. No longer did they have to rely on hand-me-downs, instead they could opt for the latest and greatest designs to furnish a whole room.

The 50s form the backbone of vintage home-style today. The designs are the starting point for many people and is an easy style to replicate. Items from the period are in demand and more trendy than ever before. Enthusiasts are lured by iconic designs and kitsch classics, which ultimately means prices are getting higher, although if you look in the right places there are still little gems out there.

The things I love most about the 50s are the kooky designs on fabrics and ceramics. I also love the furniture with its fantastic shapes and atomic age influences. If you want to create a quirky, bright and colourful statement in your home, choose the 1950s.

1950s Key Inspirations

- Design festivals
- Americana
- Rock 'n' roll music
- Travel and machines
- Science and the Atomic Age

MAIN DESIGN INFLUENCES

Atomic Age

Atomic Age design was popular during the 1950s with the use of atomic motifs and space age symbols on textiles, tables, wallpaper and ceramics. Look for space age influences that were being featured for the first time with star and galaxy motifs appearing with atomic graphics.

Contemporary Design

Influences from exhibitions and festivals of design and innovation created the demand for contemporary design in the home. Many key pieces of furniture, textiles and ceramics designed in the 50s can be a starting point to getting this slightly more sleek and functional look.

Classic Kitsch

Kitsch is a style that describes things that were cheaply mass-produced, such as artwork, furniture and ornaments. Many of these items are actually now considered classics of the 50s. Creating a bar area in your living room is not out of the question if you decide on a kitsch look.

Americana

Rock 'n' roll music, films and cars are great inspiration for an American 50s-style room. Take a look at American diners for kitchen style, jukeboxes with neon colours, and Hawaiian-inspired objects to create that Tiki look.

If you want to have fun with your rooms, or love primary and pastel colours as well as quirky patterns, the 50s are perfect for you.

Page 87: Emma and Nigel are big fans of the 50s and enjoy living in their Tiki and Atomic-inspired house.

Left: It's all in the detail – this modern light fitting looks great with a 50s-style surround.

Opposite: Original 1950s living room interior.

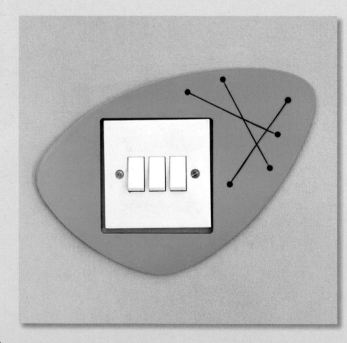

Designers and artists of the 50s

- Charles and Ray Eames – furniture
- Lucienne Day – textiles
- Arne Jacobsen – chairs
- Robin Day – furniture
- Jackson Pollock – abstract art

Left: An original Formica sideboard and checkerboard flooring are perfect for a retro-style kitchen.

Opposite: This original 1950s American wallpaper was a rare find and works well with the other original items in this dining area.

1950S DETAILS

Walls

Wallpaper was very popular. Often one wall would be a feature with a striking pattern, with the other walls papered in a colour to match, but with less or no pattern. For a kitsch or Atomic look go for quirky patterned wallpaper with motifs or scenes. The contemporary look for wallpaper was muted grey or mustard yellow, more understated but effective. For modern alternatives see Sanderson.

Textiles

Some 50s textiles are very sought-after. Designs from Lucienne Day, Jacqueline Groag and Marian Mahler are like gold dust. They were produced by manufacturers such as David Whitehead and Heals Fabrics.

Keep patterned fabrics to curtains or cushions, as upholstery on chairs and sofas was plain. Whimsical and abstract forms with strong contrasting colours are typical of fabrics from this period. Food and drink, botanical and atomic motifs were often used, and these are great for impact.

TOP TIP

Look closely, as unused examples of these striking fabrics might have the designer's and manufacturer's names printed on a white strip along the edge, known as the selvedge, which is a perfect reference to date a design.

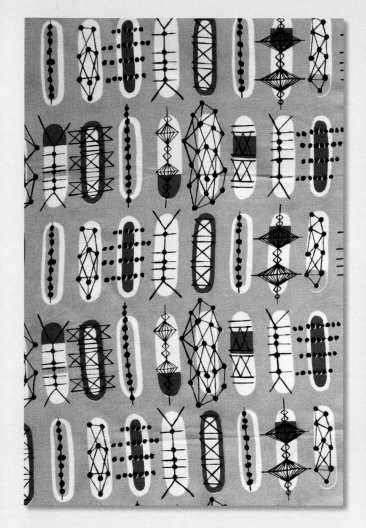

Above: Even tea towels featured quirky patterns.

Above: Fantastic Atomic styling on this heavy linen fabric. The designer is unknown but this piece is very similar to textiles produced by the David Whitehead factory in the 1950s.

Opposite top: Typical 1950s kitchen curtains with a botanical theme.

Opposite bottom: Novelty print fabric was very popular in this bright optimistic decade.

Furniture

You can't go wrong if you look for what I describe as 'kick out legs' – most kitsch and contemporary furniture from the 50s had these splayed legs. Shapes were quirky: look for kidney-shaped side tables, or boomerang-shaped coffee tables for the kitsch look. Wooden armchairs and room dividers offer a contemporary look. New plastics such as Formica and melamine were inexpensive and available in a variety of patterns and colours – look for tables, sideboards and bedroom furniture. To really make a statement get a cocktail bar – great for parties!

Far left: Old advert for G-Plan, Texturide-covered, faux leather chairs, sofas and footstools. The advert appeared in a magazine in 1956.

Left: A 1950s German plant stand.

Below left: Ercol coffee table with classic splayed legs and a selection of Hornsea pottery.

Right: An original bamboo bar with a selection of barware.

Accessories

You can have lots of fun with accessories in your 1950s home. This was a new prosperous era and lots of articles were being mass-produced. Look out for household items with the atomic round ball on the end of hooks or legs, often found on magazine racks, coat hooks or plant holders. A record player was a common household item, and the name to look for is Dansette in two-tone colours – they often came on splayed legs too. Many 50s ceramics such as vases and plates can be easily found. Also look for wall plaques and ornamental cats and poodles.

Artwork

Artwork was abstract or mass-market kitsch, many people had classic images above their fireplace or in the bedroom. Jackson Pollock pioneered abstract drip paintings and you may be able to find similar prints. Kitsch art is not everyone's cup of tea, but prints by Tretchikoff are styles to look out for. In particular, keep your eyes peeled for *Chinese Girl* (see example on page 107) or *Miss Wong*.

Lighting

Lights were fun as well as functional and there are plenty of styles to choose from. Wall lights with decorated glass shades are great for the bedroom. Sculptural contemporary lighting would suit a more sleek style. Atomic- or Sputnik-inspired lights are classic 1950s – look out for table lamps that look like flying saucers! You can also have fun with novelty American lamps made from plaster depicting oriental ladies, poodles or dancers.

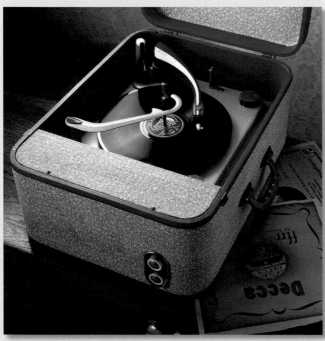

Left: Kitsch 1950s Chalkware lamp.

Opposite top: An ashtray with atomic round balls on the end of long legs.

Opposite bottom: Dansette record player.

97

GET THE LOOK: 1950S

Creating a 50s home offers the chance to design rooms using fun fabrics and wallpapers, and quirky furniture. There was a bright optimistic feel to this decade and the boom in labour-saving devices (as well as babies!) gave this era's homes a very happy vibe.

Look out for free-form organic shapes and splayed legs on furniture to create an instant 50s feel. The 50s were fun, so this is your chance to inject some personality into your home by going for kitsch items that make for instant talking points.

KITCHEN

The 50s kitchen was evolving. Early in the decade many kitchens were still a small separate room filled with separate free-standing pieces of furniture or units. This style of kitchen with its sparse layout existed from the 20s to the early 50s and had not really changed in all this time. Now, labour-saving appliances were coming onto the market, such as fridges, cookers and washing machines, and fitted kitchens were slowly being introduced. If you were lucky enough to have one, you were the envy of your street.

The use of primary colours in a kitchen is a key tip for creating that 50s style. Try red, blue or yellow and pair with a black and white chequerboard floor. Key accessories and finding the right units will help to achieve this look.

Above: An original kitchen step-stool by popular kitchen accessories maker 'Prestige' and original fridge.

Opposite: An original 1950s American Dinette set in mint green.

What to Look For: 50s Kitchen

- Abstract design Formica table and matching chairs
- Formica side unit
- Food and drink motif curtains
- Worcester ware storage tins
- Freestanding kitchen unit with dropdown front and storage cupboards
- American 50s-style fridge
- Classic food mixer
- Fold-out kitchen step-stools

Kitchen Units and Tables

Most of us nowadays will have a fitted kitchen, so it's a bit extreme to rip it out and start from scratch to create a 50s look. But if you are up for that and have the cash required, then get the epitome of 50s kitchens installed: an English Rose kitchen! They were described in their original advert as 'a built-in appearance that adds beauty to the most important room in the house' and I agree, they are a British design classic. After the war, CSA Industries Ltd launched this first 'fitted kitchen', made from the same aluminium that was used to make WWII aeroplanes,

If your budget won't stretch to this Rolls Royce of kitchens, there are some great alternative kitchen larder units to be found. With cupboards, drop-down worktops and drawers they offer storage, but also really set the scene in any 50s style kitchen!

Finally you may have the space for a Formica table and chairs or dinette. Formica was a durable work surface invented in the 50s that could be created with abstract patterns typical of the era. Many of these tables fold down and can be tucked away, or you could go for an American dinette with metal legs to create that American diner look.

Top: English Rose badge which can be found on all CSA units.

Left: A good example of mixing old and new. This modern kitchen has a great retro look to tie in with the original items.

Opposite: Jennifer and Martin sourced their original English Rose kitchen over 20 years ago at a bargain price and it fits really well into the space.

Kitchen accessories and bakeware

Start by finding 1950s storage tins – they come in some fantastic designs in classic 50s primary colours. They were durable so there are still lots of them around, but they are extremely sought-after, so expect to pay up to £30 each for rare examples. Condition can vary, as they were well-used everyday items. I love 1950s kitchen tins as the designs are amazing and illustrate the period perfectly! Look out for Worcester Ware – they made tea, cake and biscuit tins among other things.

Tala is a very good name to look out for in 50s bakeware, they produced cooks measures, flour shakers and whisks: vital requirements for any 50s housewife.

Many people opted for the new-fangled plastic melamine. Available in bright colours it was a practical alternative to the traditional stoneware ranges being mass-produced.

Top: American mid-century designed plate called North Star by Salem Pottery.

Left: 1950s Atomic towel rail with various tea towels.

Opposite: This Dazey ice crusher, styled to look like a rocket, in its original packaging looks too good to use.

Crockery

Fifties pottery is a subject I could talk about all day! There were so many different and fantastic pottery makers emerging in the 50s. However, when it comes to kitchen crockery, there are one or two classics that you could start to collect and display in your kitchen.

Homemaker from Ridgway Potteries is an outright winner for the 50s look. It was mass-produced and sold by Woolworths from the mid 50s, designed to appeal to young people setting up home for the first time. Look out for plates, bowls and the elusive tea pot. Other cool makers to look out for include T.G. Green, Beswick, Alfred Meakin, Midwinter, Kathie Winkle and quite a few Scandinavian potteries. The list is vast and they could all be used to adorn walls and shelves all over your home, not just the kitchen!

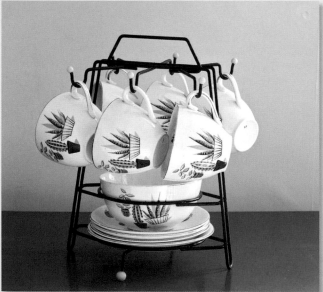

Top: Collect a selection of 50s ceramics to set the scene in your kitchen. Front: Homemaker Metro coffee pot and oval plate designed by Enid Seeney. Back: Midwinter 'Zambesi' coffee pot designed by Jessie Tate.

Left: A fantastic tea set by Alfred Meakin called 'Cactus' with a neat Atomic metal display rack.

Opposite: Grouping various plate designs together makes a cheerful wall feature. These designs all have great names: Homemaker, Fiesta, Fantasia, Parisienne and Nature Study.

LIVING ROOM

A fifties living room can include very contrasting styles, contemporary or kitsch, and I want to explore the extremes that can both look fab in the right house, whether you want a classic and contemporary room or a fun and quirky space. At the start of the 50s the living room was still quite formal, but as prosperity grew and influences came through from new designers the living room was one of the key spaces to be transformed.

Younger families who took inspiration from the Festival of Britain were looking for contemporary spaces. 'Through' lounges were common, creating an open feeling, although people still defined spaces into those for seating and dining.

You can give your living room a 50s feel with just a few key pieces of classic kitsch for a fun look. Or take inspiration from the key designers from this era and go for a contemporary, more minimalist style.

What to Look For: 50s Living Room

- High backed armchairs and sofa with splayed legs
- Atomic-patterned curtains
- Feature wallpaper
- Quirky plant stand
- Wire magazine rack
- Boomerang-shaped side table
- Starburst clock
- Cocktail bar (optional)
- Print by Tretchikoff

Above: 50s-style modern sofa, original kitsch picture and sewing box with kick-out legs create a mid-century look.

Left: A starburst clock design, popular from the 50s–70s. This teak one is by Seth Thomas.

Opposite: This Vladimir Tretchikoff print of 'Chinese Girl' looks at home on this striking teak sideboard.

Catherine and Stephen's 50s, 60s and 70s style

" We're big fans of simple design and smooth lines with masses of functionality and think most classics from the Midcentury have both in bucket loads. We like to mix Midcentury with modern and classic designs. "

Seating

It's important to get this right. It was popular in the 50s to have wingback armchairs and sofas with splayed legs. They were covered in reasonably plain woven fabrics, often in contrasting two-tone shades. Nowadays it's probably wise to have a mixture of old and new seating, as some of the original chairs look great, but may not be as well-padded and comfortable as their modern counterparts.

Famous designers of the time were Charles and Ray Eames, and British designer Robin Day, who created beautiful lounge chairs and statement pieces, that would have only been found in the wealthiest households. There was also a wave of Scandinavian designers coming through like Arne Jacobsen and Hans Wegner and their popularity and inspiration continued into the 60s.

I have two modern 50s-inspired sofas with kick-out legs. They look the part, but I suspect they are more comfortable than originals. Look out for names like Ercol, Parker Knoll and G-plan, all of which offer good examples of armchairs from the 50s. Complement your seating with a footstool in a similar style and sit back and relax.

Above: Scandinavian-style teak rocking chair.

Opposite: Retro living room with teak sofa and 1950s Dutch Tomado shelving unit.

109

Bar

It's fair to say not everyone will fancy a bar in the corner of their living room, but why ever not?! Having one, if your living space allows, will certainly give you the kitsch/tiki style you might crave.

Bars came in various shapes and sizes, but whatever their design they were certainly not understated. They were popular in the 50s and 60s, but some of the 50s ones are the best examples. Topped off with a pineapple ice bucket, some Babycham glasses and various other quirky 50s bar paraphernalia you will be ready to entertain at any time.

What to Look For: 50s Hallway

- Atomic coat hooks
- Umbrella stand
- Telephone table

Left: A great idea for a shoe rack, making use of a pair of 50s splayed legs.

Opposite: A collection of pineapples, perfect for a kitsch bar. The ones here include an ice bucket, cocktail sticks and glass holders.

What to Look For: 50s Bedroom

- Light oak bedroom furniture with splayed legs
- Goblin Teasmade
- Kitsch poodle lamp
- Ottoman with kick-out legs
- Atomic style mirror
- Round wicker or plastic chair
- Ceramic wall plaques of ladies faces
- Cantilever wooden sewing box

Left: 1950s artwork with a bamboo frame.

Opposite: Pretty pink bedroom with original and reproduction Atomic features from America, including a pair of repro 'amoeba' shadow boxes displaying original planters.

Emma and Nigel's 50s-style home

" *We love the flamboyancy, mix of shapes, pattern, colours and textures of the 1950s, as well as the kitsch elements, which aimed to create a fun style after the drabness of wartime.* "

What to Look For: 50s Bathroom

- Mirrored bathroom cabinet
- Two-tone tiles as a splash back above the sink
- Worcester ware metal bin
- Storage jars – kitchen ceramics can be used for the bathroom as storage
- Atomic hooks on the back of the door
- Barkcloth curtains in abstract pattern
- Chance glass vase
- Roberts radio

1960s Home

This was a decade of major change. The 60s ended very differently to how they began, due to liberating and positive changes in attitudes, technology and world affairs.

There is a fab saying about the 60s – 'if you remember them, you weren't there' – which sums up a lot about the time. This era was a young person's playground, offering greatly increased social freedom. It was a time of self-expression and trend-setting. Major changes in music created a new style of 'pop' music, and revolutionary fashion played a big part in how homes were starting to look.

Foreign travel was also becoming more widespread and the arrival of package holidays meant that more people could get away and explore new countries, with the ability to bring back souvenirs, ornaments and artwork to adorn their homes.

Style within the home changed at a pace in this era, so there is a cornucopia of choice in design influences when creating a 60s pad! The previous decade's love of American design was replaced, as Swinging London became the centre of all things groovy.

Space was a great inspiration for everyday home items and the use of 'throwaway' materials gave flexibility to the way rooms were arranged. Plastic was widely used to create unique shapes for chairs, tables and storage.

Colour was vital, not only because the first colour TVs became widely available, but a vibrant splash of the bright and the bold created a very groovy feel to living spaces. It was anything but bland.

For me the psychedelic colours and flower power patterns that can be found on fabric and pottery from this era are inspirational. It's fair to say that the 60s influence my choices in fashion and home furnishings more than any other decade. I am attracted to bright objects; like a magpie to shiny things!

If you want to create a really cool and fun style for your house, choose the 1960s.

1960s Key Inspirations
- The Space Race
- Popular films
- Art and design
- Pop music
- Flower Power

MAIN DESIGN INFLUENCES

Scandinavian

Until the mid 60s the prevailing style took influences from Scandinavian chic. Furniture had clean, sharp lines, with influences from designers from Denmark, Finland and Norway creating sculptural seating, striking ceramics and beautiful glass as well as functional and well-crafted kitchenware.

Pop

Pop Art style took inspiration from comics and popular culture. Check out Andy Warhol's *Campbell's Soup Cans* for the most iconic reference. Modern art with geometric shapes and vibrant colours decorated homes, as well as psychedelic prints, optical art-style textiles and wall coverings.

Space Age

This style drew upon the Space Race and films of the time. Take a look at the sets of James Bond films and *Barbarella*. Space age styles were white, silver and black, creating a futuristic feel, which was popularised by Mary Quant and the Mod look.

Page 115: Catherine and Stephen like to mix items from different decades in their home but do love a lot of stylish designs from the 60s.

Right: Original 1960s bedroom design.

Designers of the 60s
- Vernon Panton – chairs
- Andy Warhol – art
- Mary Quant – fashion and textiles
- Terence Conran – design

1960S DETAILS

Walls

For an early 60s Scandinavian look try a feature wall of exposed brick or wood panelling. There are plenty of companies who reproduce 1960s-style wallpaper or you might be able to find enough of an original pattern to create a feature wall or even frame large pieces. Look for geometric or flower patterns. It was very popular to have white painted walls, the perfect backdrop to lots of cool groovy artwork.

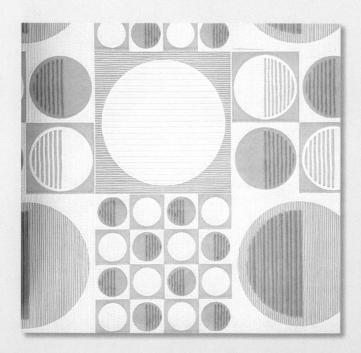

Left: This textured wall effect was created using slate tiles and gives a similar look to exposed brick.

Opposite: A selection of groovy wallpaper samples.

Lisa and Dan's 60s-style home

" *We're never done searching. Dan is a chair nut and would love more room for design-classic chairs in the house. Lisa is like a magnet for other's castaways and forgotten trinkets.* "

Textiles

Search for unused original textiles; they can be picked up very easily. Textiles manufacturers such as Hull Traders, Heals and Edinburgh Weavers led the way in developing op art and abstract prints designed by artists of the time.

Make curtains – bold patterns will make an impact – or cover chairs or cushions. Even if you have a modern sofa, the choice of fabric can tie in a look. Think about framing pieces of fabric that match your colour sceme to bring your room together.

Top: Original linen Flower Power fabric.

Left: Mary Quant tablecloth.

Opposite: Lisa and Dan wanted to create a fun home inspired by the bright and vibrant colours of the 60s.

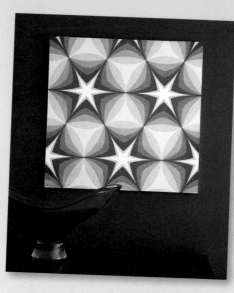

TOP TIP

Make your own wall art by gluing a piece of original wallpaper to a piece of hardboard and hanging it.

Artwork

In the 60s, there was lots of mass market artwork being produced and sold in home stores. Look out for Andy Warhol-style prints or geometric op art for a pop look. Alternatively, choose something more mass market like a classic of the 60s – good examples are artworks from J. H. Lynch who produced a series of sultry-looking ladies such as *Tina* and *Autumn Leaves*. On the other hand create your own art from 60s magazine covers or adverts, or pieces of fabric stretched over a frame.

Right: Set of three kistch children's artworks.

Opposite: Artist J.H. Lynch's *Autumn Leaves* print.

Accessories

Plastic was truly fantastic in the 60s, and mirrors, telephones, kitchen items and magazine racks made from various coloured plastics are good for styling.

A radiogram or portable radio is a great accessory – search for household names such as Bush, Roberts or Pye.

Sixties glassware came in organic shapes. Adorn shelves and sideboards with Murano glass vases and bowls in two-tone colours.

Lighting

There is a fantastic range of iconic lighting to choose from for a 60s home. Lighting was space-aged; the rocket lamp was a feature in many living rooms.

In 1963 the Lava Lamp was launched and the same company are still producing them in psychedelic colours today.

Plastic pendant shades that were mushroom-shaped in black, silver or white were a new style and these can often be found at big antiques markets.

Top: 1960s orange plastic clock.

Left: Orange spun-fibre rocket lamp with teak legs.

Opposite: Reproduction of an Eero Aarnio Globe or Ball chair.

GET THE LOOK: 1960S

Creating a 60s home gives the option of two contrasting styles: the sleek and stylish early part of the decade, versus the hip and far-out later years.

Don't clutter rooms with too many decorative items, which is tempting as 60s items are quite easy to source. There is a fine line between creating a styled home and a cluttered one. Remember, the 60s were supposed to be minimalist – open-plan living is the look.

KITCHEN

Full of built-in cupboards for maximum storage, the fitted kitchen had arrived on the mass market. They were kitted out with a vast array of labour-saving devices and appliances to make cooking and entertaining easier. Electric toasters, kettles and even fondue pots were must-haves, offering a talking point at an ultra-sophisticated soirée.

Kitchens of this era offered a more pleasurable environment in which to cook, feeling less like a place for chores. They were a space to spend time in and experiment with exotic recipes and foods, as entertaining was a very popular pastime.

The style and functionally of the 60s kitchen was quite a lot like our modern-day kitchens, so creating a 60s style is quite easy to achieve. An open-plan layout is perfect and, using the right accessories, will still be achievable even in the smallest of spaces.

Left: Original 1960s kitchen design.

Opposite: The use of vibrant colours and bold patterns pulls together an exciting 60 look in this kitchen.

Storage Jars and Cookware

Storage jars and cookware can be found quite easily at fairs and markets. Not only are they practical additions, they instantly give a visual look to a kitchen too. Go for bold colours like orange, cobalt blue or lime green – many of these colours featured on storage jars and cookware from the 60s. Look out for ranges from Taunton Vale, Hornsea and Nelson Pottery.

Don't shut your saucepans away, use them to decorate shelves. Look out for flower power or psychedelic designs to brighten up worktops. Alternatively take inspiration from the earlier part of the decade and opt for a more sleek Scandinavian style like Norwegian cookware factory Catherineholm, with its ever-popular Lotus range of pots and pans.

Top: Portmerion Pottery 'Talisman' and Taunton Vale 'Daisy' storage jars.

Left: Catherineholm Cookware was produced in Norway and the most popular design is this Lotus pattern. Hardwearing and usable it is very collectable and perfect for a mid-century style kitchen.

Opposite: Crown Devon Flower Power storage jars.

Left: A Midwinter 'Spanish Garden' dinner service.

Opposite: A selection of Lord Nelson 'Gaytime' serving jars.

Tableware and Crockery

The 60s offered a plethora of tableware and crockery to choose from, and these were quite often bought as wedding presents. As entertaining became a popular activity there were lots of companies offering well-styled serving dishes, teapots, plates and condiments.

Pottery manufacturers employed modern designers, favouring screen-printing instead of hand painting which allowed bold decoration and cutting-edge designs to reach the masses. Look for the Midwinter Focus pattern designed by Barbara Brown, a textile designer of the time, or Midwinter Spanish Garden.

When it comes to picking up pieces today it is pretty straightforward. Go with your heart, what catches your eye and suits your budget. Keep your eye out for names like Midwinter and Portmeirion who created a broad range of dinner services and crockery with many wonderfully colourful patterns. Some of it is iconic of the period, which means they can be a little bit pricey. Don't worry: many others such as J. & G. Meakin and Washington potteries can be found at minimal cost and give a great and immediate 60s zing, raising admiring glances from all your friends.

My everyday tableware is the Sienna design by Midwinter, they look as vibrant today as when I bought them at a flea market years ago.

What To Look For: 60s Kitchen/Dining Room

- White kitchen units can offer a blank canvas for an injection of colour and pattern
- Go for chrome or steel fittings, to bring out the space age feel
- Round white table and stacking coloured dining chairs from moulded plastic
- 1960s radio – Bush or Roberts
- Arco style floor light
- Orange wall clock
- Bright coloured storage jars and saucepans
- Flower pottery – Figgjo Flint 'Daisy', Lord Nelson 'Gaytime' or Taunton Vale.

DINING SPACE

The dinner party was born, homes were open-plan and very sociable, and cookery programmes started on TV. Holding a dinner party was a chance to show off not only your culinary delights, but also your new dining table and dinner service to the neighbours.

If you have an open kitchen-diner you are halfway there. However you may only have a small space within your kitchen for eating or a separate dining space, either way you can get a 60s look to suit your budget.

Seating

Finding the right type of dining table and chairs to fit your space is crucial. For a smaller space try a Formica table and chairs, which were still in fashion in the 60s. These often have handy drawers underneath for extra storage and can fold down out of the way. Choose a bright primary colour such as yellow or red that complements your kitchen accessories.

A bigger space gives you the option to make a statement. Go for a white space-age, round table and chairs, my favourite look of the 60s. Alternatively hunt down a teak table, many of these can seat up to 6 or 8 people. Make a central feature of it, don't put it up against the wall. You could even dress it with nice pieces of glassware while not in use.

Names to look out for are the Arkana Tulip table and chairs, which are white and made from fibreglass, but they may be pricey, so look out for cheaper alternatives that were made by shops like Habitat. For the Scandinavian look go for teak furniture by Nathan, McIntosh or G-Plan. For a lighter look choose Ercol, as this was mass-produced and is still easily available. If you want to splash out I would recommend you buy an investment piece. Do a search for Danish Teak tables and take a look at the one designed by Hans Olsen for Frem Rojle, which is particular favourite of mine. The table extends, but the chairs fit away under the table, a great space-saving design.

Right: Get the space-aged look with a 60s style Tulip table and Eiffel chairs – these are reproductions.

Opposite: Retro dining room with original Frem Rojle table.

Lighting

Lighting can set the mood in a dining space, so pick something that makes an immediate impact. Pendant lamps and mushroom-shaped shades are an easy way to add a focal point. Arco floor lamps are a classic as they create a great feature light in the middle of a dining table. Go for bright colours like orange if you are creating a pop art look, white or silver for a space-age feel, and for the Scandinavian style choose a sleek and simple pendant with natural wood and metal features.

When buying any lighting for your home make sure you get it checked independently by an electrician and rewired if necessary.

Left: Look out for a mushroom-shaped Guzzini-style floor or table lamp like this one.

Opposite left: White 1960s plastics are useful in the bathroom. This round mirror teamed with funky wallpaper gives a standard bathroom that groovy edge.

Opposite right: Bright clashing colours and accessories make a bold statement in this bedroom. Check out the great use of old drawers lined with wallpaper to display collections of retro glass.

What to Look For: 60s Bathroom

- Plastic laundry bin with bold flower pattern
- Funky wallpaper feature wall
- Plastic framed wall mirror
- Bright towels to match the colour scheme

What to Look For: 60s Bedroom

- Lava Lamp
- Big Ben alarm clock
- White plastic round mirror
- Round wicker bedroom chair
- G-Plan style dressing table
- Flower power curtains

135

LIVING ROOM

During the 60s this room became a functional, multi-purpose space with the TV as the new focal point instead of the fireplace, similar to how it is today. A lot more time was now spent in the living room, therefore they were less formal and a place to relax.

Furniture had an important role in the living room and certain pieces of furniture had various uses. Wall-hanging display units had built in writing desks. Sofas folded out into beds. Coffee tables and footstools came with storage compartments. People were ordering furniture from mail order catalogues and going to off-the-shelf stores like Habitat. Whatever space you have to create a 60s living room, remember to create a feeling of space and light.

What to Look For: 60s Living Room

- Statement white globe or egg chair, Eero Aarnio style
- G-Plan Astro table
- Andy Warhol-inspired wall art – soup cans, comic strips, images of icons like Marilyn Monroe
- Shattaline lamp made from resin in blue, green or orange
- Psychedelic rug with swirls of bright colours
- Corner sofa with lots of bright flower power cushions
- Plain white walls allow you to display statement artwork
- Beanbags offer extra seating for guests and give a chilled 60s vibe
- Collect coloured glass vases – Holmegaard, Whitefriars and Murano styles are cool

Left: Charles & Ray Eames-style lounger.

Opposite: A wall-hanging display unit offers plenty of storage and display space, this one was made by Nisse Strinning.

Seating

Armchairs and sofas in the early 60s had an emphasis on style rather than comfort. They were made in matching colours rather than the contrasting colours of the 50s. Daybeds were pretty popular offering a practical dual purpose after late-night dinner parties. Loungers were also very popular. American designers Eames and Robin Day produced desirable examples of these with accompanying footstools in the mid sixties.

In the late 60s seating was still influenced by Scandinavian designers like Verner Panton and Eero Aarnio. Designs made from fibre glass and plastic, these were quite expensive to buy and often featured on the sets of films and TV series of the time. Chair design became very far-out, influenced by the pop culture of the mid-sixties, including blow up chairs and even ones made of cardboard, but this phase didn't last. My suggestion would be to go for a statement chair or two. Again, sleek and teak for an early 60s style or something more James Bond-like, such as the swivel Egg Chair.

Top: Teak G-Plan nest of tables.

Right: Teak G-Plan oval Astro table.

138

Right: Statement chairs can pull a room together, look for something like this Eero Saarinen 'Womb Chair'.

Sideboard and Display Units

Traditionally sideboards were used to keep cocktail glasses, bottles of Babycham and maybe your best china. Just like the dining tables of the era they were teak, rosewood or elm and were most commonly found in the dining area.

Nowadays the 60s sideboard can be the most useful piece of storage in a living room. Use it as the focal point of the room or as a practical place to stand your TV. Make use of its storage opportunities to house CDs and things you want out of the way. My sideboard is full of random things that have no other home, but are very useful all the same.

If you want to display a collection of 60s glass or pottery then why not look for a Ladderax unit. They were another popular storage solution for 60s homemakers and can offer both display space and somewhere to hide paperwork.

Top: Orange lamp made from resin by Shattaline Ltd with a fibreglass shade.

Left: A collection of teak antelope grouped together. These can be found in various sizes.

Opposite: These beautiful modernist-style Hornsea anvil vases were designed by John Clappison.

What to Look For: 60s Home Office
- Plastic desk calendar
- Funky clock with oversized numbers
- Large dial telephone
- Typewriter
- Executive desk toy – Newton's Cradle

Above: Teak mirrors are a great buy and can be used in various rooms around the house. This one has a cool abstract shape common in the 60s.

Above right: The front three are Bullet vases made by Czech factory Sklo Union and designed by Rudolf Schrotter. Lots of glass was produced in the 60s – it's not always easy to identify but if you love it, don't worry too much – just enjoy it.

Opposite: A selection of bright glass vases, including two Riihimaki vases (front and back), which were made in Finland in the 1960s.

TOP TIP
Group together similar coloured glass vases on white shelves or in alcoves to create a bold focal point.

1970s Home

This is the final vintage era to embrace and one whose style has been mocked by some, but appreciated by many as it enjoys a resurrection in modern interior style. The 70s is an era of the not-too-distant past and most of us will know someone who experienced 70s decor in all its glory.

The 70s was the first decade of the flexible friend – the credit card made buying whatever you wanted very easy and allowed for wild extravagance. The early 70s saw a crescendo to the two previous decades of growth and prosperity, before heading for a fall towards the end of the decade.

This feeling of financial times a-changing led many people to think of their homes as an investment and financial security. Many embarked on home improvement projects, extensions and redecorating, which led to an influx of do-it-yourself stores.

When I asked my parents about their first home together, they told me it contained a purple and orange living room, with a vinyl sofa and teak sideboard. If only they still had all this now to pass down, as this all sounds pretty cool to me.

It was the beginning of the computer age, but households did not enjoy this technological breakthrough for themselves until the 80s. Instead they invested in microwave ovens, music systems and video players, which were costly items at the time, but with many more women going out to work there were two incomes coming in for the first time.

A new mix of music genres hit this decade, most significantly Rock, Punk and Disco. The uber-cool spent Saturday nights at the disco getting into the groove, surrounded by glitter balls and flashing lights. The desire for a disco party pad encouraged similar lighting, hi-fi systems and glossy metal furniture – people loved a good house party.

I love the 70s mainly for the colour orange and its zingy zesty appeal. Creating a 70s-style room is about taking the cool, funky bits and fitting them neatly into a modern home, leaving the rest behind.

1970s Key Inspirations

- Music – Rock and Disco
- Arts & Crafts styling
- Art Deco and
  Art Nouveau revivals
- Fashion
- Digital technology

MAIN DESIGN INFLUENCES

Retro

Funky and bright defines this style and it can cover various eras, but my vision of retro is 70s styling with oranges, browns, yellow and green – an explosion of colour and pattern coupled with teak furniture that was more imposing than during the 60s. This style is easy to replicate as there are plenty of pieces around.

Bohemian

An eclectic bohemian ethnic look, with sheepskin rugs, bead curtains and wall hangings were inspired by free spirits and women's liberation. There was a huge revival in Arts & Crafts styling as well as Art Deco and Art Nouveau influences. This style mixed old 20s and 30s pieces with new seating such as beanbags, rattan chairs and low level sofas.

Chintz

Laura Ashley brought about the idea of the co-ordinated look when she introduced wallpapers and matching fabric in floral patterns. This chintz look was popular at the back end of the decade for the middle classes. The look worked well with country-style furniture like polished pine tables, dressers and cottage-style sofas, creating a romantic and nostalgic style.

Designers of the 70s

- Laura Ashley – soft furnishing and décor
- Barbara Hulanicki – Biba fashion
- Clive Sinclair – technology innovator
- Terence Conran – Habitat interiors shop

Page 145: This disco room sums up what's groovy about the 1970s.

Opposite: The 70s colour pallette of muted browns and vibrant flashes of colour work well with the textured shagpile rug and sheepskin cushions in this living room.

1970S DETAILS

Walls

Wallpaper was all the rage. Flowers and geometric styles remained from the 60s, getting bigger and bolder in the 70s. I would suggest you just go for a feature wall so that it does not take over the room. If you don't want a bold pattern think about paisley or ethnic patterned wallpaper or even textured effects, but stay away from the dreaded woodchip, that will never have its day again! Plain magnolia, light brown or muted yellow walls would be a good backdrop allowing you to go wild with textiles. For a bedroom you could choose purples or lilacs, using orange as an accent for accessories.

Top left: An example of original paisley wallpaper.

Left: Flower patterns continued into 70s homes and this bright design would be perfect in a kitchen or bathroom.

Opposite: This wall is covered with a large bold 70s pattern mixing brown with zingy yellow and orange.

Textiles

Textiles offered a range of extremes in the 70s from the obvious far-out and funky riot of colour, via the Art Nouveau revived prints introduced by London-based fashion and household accessories shop Biba, to the end of the 70s Laura Ashley chintzy florals. Man-made fabrics allowed cheaper printing allowing more people could be bold with textiles. These fabrics are easy to find, but they may cause friction – literally! Some of these nylon and polyester textiles have the most amazing patterns though, so don't be deterred.

Above: A piece of 1970s curtain fabric.

Left: A swinging bamboo 'parrot' basket chair with a sheepskin rug are perfect for the bedroom or living room for a bohemian look.

Artwork

The style of artwork was diverse, taking inspiration from Art Deco and Art Nouveau revivals as well as geometric and ethnic designs. Look for prints by Alphonse Mucha.

Shops such as Athena were opening in Britain offering inexpensive artwork and posters to a mass market. Lots of people made their own art from kits. Pin and thread craft was a popular pastime, and you can pick up these pictures quite easily, often featuring butterflies or abstract shapes.

Above: Handcrafts were a popular pastime in the 70s. Here are two examples of handmade pincraft pictures.

Right: Orange was a key colour spanning the 60s and 70s. You can't go wrong with artwork using tones of orange in your home.

Stuart and Louise's 70s-style home

" We firmly believe 'they don't make them like they used to.' We find most of today's affordable furniture and decoration poorly made and boring. For the same price you can have a designer item from the 70s, which looks stunning. We see it as an investment. "

Accessories

Many home accessories in the 70s were textured and tactile. Rugs were thick and fluffy plus there were lots of cushions and throws. The houseplant was a popular feature of the 1970s home and the macramé plant holder featured as a passing fashion. New technology was everywhere and the man of the house enjoyed a space for the hi-fi and for video games to be played.

Lighting

Hanging globes and dome lights were still influencing the style of lighting in the 70s. Teak lighting with glass fittings was still popular. Chrome is a style to look for too, either floor-standing lamps or table lamps. Fibre optic lights were a new invention, bul were very expensive to buy until the 80s.

Right: House plants were extremely popular in the 70s. Often ferns, spider plants or mother-in-law's tongues were dotted around every room.

Opposite: Stuart and Louise have a fabulous collection of high-end furniture from manufacturer British Pieff. This sideboard is part of the Pieff range designed by Tim Bates. The sideboards were only made to order and mainly sold in Harrods or Heals.

GET THE LOOK: 1970S

Take all the cool bits of the 1970s and bring them together to create a tasteful look back at an era that many of us remember from the first time round, or at least know somebody who does. This disco decade can offer a funky party pad with lots of masculine touches of technology, or a laidback chilled atmosphere with muted tones of cream and brown with a textured, touchy-feely vibe. Use accent colours like orange, green or yellow with more muted tones to give a sophisticated look. Finding cool and interesting 70s pieces is easy, you may even have relatives who have things in their loft or garage, so ask around. Go for well made classics.

LIVING ROOM

The 70s living room was designed to be comfortable and relaxed. Sunken seating areas and open-plan living with large feature fireplaces were high fashion. However, digging a hole in your living room to create a sunken seating area is a bit extreme. Look for low level furniture and rich materials, and create the wow factor with a statement shagpile rug.

Opposite: More high-end Pieff furniture from the Mandarin range, as well as a Quadrifoglio table lamp from Guzzini.

Furniture

Go for a low level sofa in brown leather with chrome arms or feet as a key piece of furniture in your living room. Velour was also a popular fabric used on seating. Look for a swivel armchair with chrome feet, they often came with matching footstools. A quick search on the Internet will give you examples from the UK and Denmark. Think about creating a relaxed seating area with beanbags, these can be bought new but give the right look.

Smoked glass was a popular look in furniture, mixed with chrome. You can find coffee tables and shelving units with this feature as well as dining tables and chairs.

What to Look For: 70s Living Room

- Shagpile rugs
- Low level sofa in leather or velour
- Groups of West German pottery
- Orange or brown iGuzzini table or floor lamp
- Smoked glass top coffee table
- Trimphone – popular design of telephone
- Chrome shelving unit
- Teak sunburst clock

Above: This yellow Weltron Space Ball Helmet 8-track player is a great example of cool gadgets and technology to have dotted around if you want a 70s look.

Right: A Componibili plastic storage unit designed by Anna Castelli Ferrieri for Kartell, and classic Trim phone.

Opposite: Look for chrome-edged furniture and shelving on which to display collections of glass and ceramics from the decade.

Accessories

Go for a teal sunburst clock in a prominent location. Look for feature lighting in orange or yellow with chrome fittings. Italian lighting from iGuzzini was popular in the 70s and these lights can be picked up from vintage interiors shops. They are an investment, but a key piece to pull a look together.

West German pottery, although it had been around in the 50s and 60s, was a popular choice in the 70s due to its textured glaze and mix of browns and creams with bright funky colours. Group together items of similar colours to get a great effect on a shelf or mantlepiece.

BEDROOM

A chilled-out space with low level furniture and mood lighting with simple details.

Bed

Seventies bedroom style was about built-in storage and low-level beds that incorporated cupboards, shelves and bedside tables as one unit. Dress the bed with simple, plain muted covers in browns and cream, using cushions to add some colour and texture. For decoration fold a more patterned 70s bedspread and place at the bottom of your bed, tying in the accent colour of your room.

Accessories

Mood lighting or even a disco ball would give a groovy look. Plastic flatpack lampshades were also used for a central ceiling fitting. Go for a blind at the windows instead of curtains and hang a macramé hanging pendant or plant holder in the corner of the room. Use sheepskin rugs for texture and a warm cosy feeling.

Choose bold bedside lights in accent colours of purple or orange. Why not have a wallhanging of brass butterflies or birds above your bed – these give a 3D effect, adding more interest than a framed picture. Finally choose a teak framed mirror for the wall.

Left: A teak bed frame with floating shelf.

Right: Rattan peacock chair and macramé lantern create a hippy chic look. Macramé was another popular hobby in the 70s. Plant holders and owl pendants were amongst the items made using cotton twine or yarn.

What to Look For: 70s Bedroom

- Sheepskin rugs
- Velour headboard, or headboard with fitted bedside tables
- Patterned bedspread for the end of the bed
- Blanket box with seat
- Flatpack lamp shades or disco ball light
- Hanging wicker 'parrot' chair or 'peacock' chair
- Macramé plant holder or pendant

What to Look For: 70s Kitchen/Dining Room

- Fondue set
- Tupperware
- Rise and Fall lamp
- Teak dropleaf or chrome and smoked glass table and chairs
- Lazy Susan for the table
- Stainless steel electric kettle
- Viners knives and forks
- Hornsea Saffron storage jars
- J. G. Meakin dinner service
- Hostess trolley for entertaining

Above: A selection of Tupperware is a useful addition to any 70s-inspired kitchen.

Left: Tea and coffee sets were often made from ironstone and are therefore more durable. This is a Staffordshire Potteries example.

Opposite: 'Fred the Flour Grader' was a character created by Homepride Flour to help promote its flour. Flour shakers, baking sets and spice racks were available to collect.

What to Look For: 70s Bathroom

- Sunken bath
- Coloured bathroom suite
- Vinyl wallpaper used on a feature wall
- Bathroom cabinet with mirrored front
- West German pottery vases and plant pots
- Ali Baba laundry basket

Right: An original vibrant yellow bath is not to everyone's taste but shows how anything goes with styling from this decade.

Opposite: The subtle use of 70s wallpaper and fabric offcuts combined with some glass and pottery from the decade work well in this bathroom.

Vintage Home Styles and Fashions

Our home styles have always been heavily influenced by fashion as tastes have changed through the decades. You may think that 'vintage' is a single term used to describe old things, which it is. It also describes various fashions and styles that come under the main umbrella 'vintage', and there are quite a few genres to get your head around.

Having guided you through the differences in each of the decades I want to give you a quick guide to the particular vintage styles that don't conform to one era, but do describe a vintage look.

SHABBY CHIC

'Shabby chic' is a term that does get used a lot when people talk about vintage. It's a style that has been around for a while and can be often seen as feminine. A true shabby chic look requires true vintage items, chintzy textiles such as patchwork quilts, eiderdowns in pastel colours, worn distressed furniture in pale tones and pretty accessories. Warning: don't go mad with bunting as it's a bit of a cliché.

You will see many 'shabby chic' reproduction items in shops from small independents to big brands, but try to avoid too much of this. Remember, vintage is about creating an individual style. Try to mix more old than new pieces to create an elegant effect.

Left: Classic floral textiles are essential for shabby chic style.

Right: Go for soft colour tones and painted furniture for this feminine look. Don't be afraid to mix different textures and patterns.

MIDCENTURY MODERN

Midcentury modern is an architecture and interior style that generally describes mid-20th century design. Think Eames, Le Corbusier, Robin Day, Herman Miller and so on. For home interiors it covers furniture, decorative items, textiles and artwork from the mid-30s to the mid-60s. This style is very sleek and sophisticated, requiring some key pieces at keen prices to pull the look off effectively.

Above left: Striking Midcentury inspired wallpaper can create a quick and instant effect and then you can build up a collection of iconic furniture as and when your budget allows.

Above right: This Eames rocker makes a great statement chair.

Opposite: Catherine and Stephen have included their son Lucas's bedroom in their Midcentury styling with touches of classic furniture, textiles and colours.

RETRO

Retro style is the funky side of the past, it's a style that seems to have many different meanings to different people, but when I describe a retro look I am talking about mixing mass-produced furniture from the 60s and 70s that still has style, with bold and bright items from the same decade. Think G-Plan sideboard, red plastic telephone and funky wallpaper. It's a fun look.

Left: The key to reto style is bright colours and cool chairs, great lighting, and mixing and matching vintage and vintage-style items.

Above: A collection of Hornsea Pottery and Carlton ware lined up.

Opposite: Mix teak and a bold feature wallpaper.

INDUSTRIAL

This is about using vintage items for a completely different use. It's stuff you would find in a reclamation yard, old factory or school. For example, old factory lights can be used for kitchen lighting, metal school lockers as storage in the bedroom or old wooden crates put together and used as a bookcase. This style is about thinking how something could be re-used to make a feature in your home.

Left: Used metal and wood are the basis of this style – look for quirky uses for objects. The machinist's chair adds lot of character and could be a good talking point if you know its origins. It would work well in a kitchen of this style.

Opposite: Old school lockers make great storage.

ECLECTIC

This style has a feeling of years of collecting quirky items from different periods, bringing them all together in a way that gives a very chic look. It's about combining a mixture of textures, time periods, styles, trends and colours. Mixing vintage and antiques from markets, with family heirlooms and brand new items is important for this look to work.

Look for things that have a lived-in feeling that may look well-worn. Don't worry about things matching – different types of woods and paint colours can be mixed up. Be mindful to get the right balance to avoid making it look too hectic. This is certainly a look you can add to as time goes on.

Left: Mix whatever quirky items you love for this look. The vintage map marries the whole style together in this kitchen.

Opposite: Simon and Nick have mixed a variety of religious artefacts with antiques, kitsch ornaments and quality textiles and wallpaper to create a beautiful effect in this bedroom.

VINTAGE SHOPS

LONDON & SOUTH

Alfies Antique Market, 13-25 Church Street, Marylebone,
   London NW8 8DT www.alfiesantiques.com
Mid20c, 63 W End, Redruth TR15 2SQ
Nanadobbie, 16 Gloucester Road, Hove, Brighton,
   East Sussex BN1 4AD www.nanadobbie.com
The Old Cinema, 160 Chiswick High Road, London W4 1PR
   www.theoldcinema.co.uk
What Katy Did, 57 High Street, Budleigh Salterton,
   Exeter EX9 6LE www.whatkatydid.biz

MIDLANDS & EAST

Boomerang Vintage & Retro, 21 The Lightworks,
   Market Street, Hednesford, Staffordshire WS12 1AD
   www.boomerangvintage.co.uk
Vintage Mischief, The Old Dairy, Hungate Lane, Beccles,
   Suffolk NR34 9TN www.vintagemischief.com
Vintage Treasures, 5 The Lawns, Hinckley, Leicestershire
   LE10 1DY www.vintage-treasures.co.uk

NORTH & SCOTLAND

Insitu, 252 Chester Road, Hulme, Manchester M15 4EX
   www.insitumanchester.com
Love Salvage, 8 Harmony Square, Govan, Glasgow G51 3LW
   www.lovesalvage.com
Space Harrogate, The Ginnel, Harrogate, North Yorkshire
   HG1 2RB www.spaceharrogate.co.uk

WEBSITES

20thC Design www.20thcdesign.com
20th Century Collector www.20thcenturycollector.com/
Country Vintage www.country-vintage.co.uk
Fish4Junk www.fish4junk.co.uk
H is for Home www.hisforhome.com
Home Sweet Home Style www.homesweethomestyle.co.uk
Pineapple Retro www.pineappleretro.co.uk
Retrolicious www.retrolicious.co.uk
Retro Mojo www.retromojo.co.uk
Retro World www.retroworldonline.co.uk
Vintage Home www.vintage-home.co.uk
Vintage Home Emporium www.vintagehomeemporium.co.uk
Vintage Home Shop www.vintagehomeshop.co.uk
Vintage Retro www.vintageretro.co.uk
Your Vintage Life www.yourvintagelife.co.uk

SPECIALISTS

Art Deco

La Belle www.labelle-artdecoandantiques.co.uk
Cloud 9 Art Deco www.cloud9artdeco.co.uk
CLO2OC www.clo2oc.com
Deco World www.deco-world.com

Industrial

May Fly Vintage www.mayflyvintage.co.uk
Source Antiques www.source-antiques.co.uk
Turner & Cox www.turnerandcox.co.uk
Vincent and Barn www.vincentandbarn.co.uk

Kitchenalia

Vintage Kitchen Store www.vintagekitchenstore.co.uk
Vintage Things Forever www.vintage-things-forever.co.uk

Midcentury Specialist

Elephant & Monkey www.elephantandmonkey.co.uk
Fragile Design www.fragiledesign.com
Kirk Modern www.kirkmodern.com
Nanadobbie www.nanadobbie.com
V is for Vintage www.visforvintage.co.uk

Specialist Fairs & Events

Arthur Swallow Fairs www.asfairs.com
International Antiques and Collectors Fairs (IACF)
   www.iacf.co.uk
Midcentury Modern Shows www.modernshows.com
The Vintage Home Show www.vintagehomeshow.co.uk
Vintage Furniture Flea www.judysvintagefair.co.uk

Vintage Artwork

AntikBar www.antikbar.co.uk
Sharrett & Reece www.sherrattandreece.co.uk
Vintage In Print www.vintageinprint.co.uk

Vintage Glass

20th Century Glass www.20thcenturyglass.com
Glass Etc www.decanterman.com
Haybarn Glass www.haybarnglass.co.uk

Vintage Textile Specialist

Antique Textile Company www.antiquetextilescompany.co.uk
Donna Flower www.donnaflower.com
Spinsters Emporium www.spinstersemporium.co.uk
Meggy Magpie www.meggymagpie.com

ACKNOWLEDGEMENTS AND THANKS

Steve Rosendale, my better half and all-round rock, without whom I could not have done this. My 16-year-old daughter Bethany for putting up with me, as well as being a budding proofreader and shoot assistant. Emily Preece-Morrison at Pavilion for guiding me through and making the book happen, as well as putting up with my silly questions. Heather Hobhouse for taking great photos and coping with me saying 'just one more shot'! Her assistant Pauline and Claire from Pavilion for moving things with no breakages. Naomi Thompson for suggesting me – I am extremely grateful and owe you a drink or two you lovely lady. Alex Stone for telling me I should grab the opportunity and Jennifer Bird for her brilliant support, insight and the loan of many great pieces. Jayne Bocking and Noel Rimmer for helping with kitchenalia. Chris Woolman for being a glass guru. Sophie Crocket from Pineapple Retro for help with kitsch ceramics. Last, but not least, the real home owners: Sue and Ian Wood, Martin and Pauline Medley-Weston, Rachel and Dave Hinchcliffe, Emma Edwards and Nigel Preston (www.missbamboo.co.uk), Simon Warner and Nick Blakey, Jennifer and Martin Bird, Catherine and Stephen Caton, Lisa Henderson, Carrie and Michael Page, Stuart and Louise Webb, who let us invade their beautiful homes to drool over their fantastic array of vintage pieces.

PICTURE CREDITS

All special photography by Heather Hobhouse except those credited below.
©: p.7 Amanda Morgan; p.17: John Heseltine/Alamy; p.25: Amoret Tanner/Alamy; p.36: Gap Interiors/Jake Fitzjones; p.47: Mary Evans Picture Library; p.48 top: Mary Evans Picture Library/John Maclellan; p.48 below: V&A Images/Alamy; p.51 top: Elizabeth Whiting & Associates/Alamy; p.51 below: Mary Evans Picture Library; p.53: Elizabeth Whiting & Associates/Alamy; p.59: wales_heritage_photos/Alamy; p.69: Jeff Morgan 16/Alamy; p.89: M&N/Alamy; p.94: M&N/Alamy; p.96: Steve Cavalier/Alamy; p.108: Gap Interiors/Douglas Gibb; p.117: Heritage Image Partnership Ltd/Alamy; p.126: imageBROKER/Alamy; p.132: Gap Interiors/Bruce Hemming – Midcentury Magazine/DAD Design; p.166: SliceofLondonLife/Alamy; p.171: Gap Interiors/Rachel Whiting.

ABOUT THE AUTHOR

Keeley Harris is a vintage store owner, blogger and event organiser, specialising in vintage fairs, who can be found online under the webname Discover Vintage. Her passion for vintage homewares started early, when her antique dealer father took her around the country as a young girl, helping to source and sell antiques. Ceramics are her particular passion. She is frequently asked to write about vintage interior styling and her work has appeared in several magazines. She lives in Leeds, which has a thriving vintage scene to rival London. She blogs as www.vintagekeeley.co.uk and can be found on Twitter @vintagekeeley.

First published in the United Kingdom in 2015 by
Pavilion
1 Gower Street, London WC1E 6HD

"Style Me Vintage" is a registered trademark of Pavilion Books Company Ltd

Text © Keeley Harris, 2015
Design and layout © Pavilion Books Company Ltd, 2015
Photography © Pavilion Books Company Ltd, except those in Picture Credits

The moral right of the authors has been asserted.

Commissioning editor: Emily Preece-Morrison
Text editor: Kate Turvey
Designer: Emma Wicks
Photographer: Heather Hobhouse

ISBN: 978-1-86205-940-5

A CIP catalogue record for this book is available from the British Library.

Colour reproduction by Rival Colour Ltd., UK
Printed and bound by 1010 Printing International Ltd, China

This book can be ordered direct from the publisher at
www.pavilionbooks.com

10 9 8 7 6 5 4 3 2 1

ALSO AVAILABLE FROM PAVILION BOOKS:

Style Me Vintage: Hair by Belinda Hay, ISBN 978-1-86205-902-3
Style Me Vintage: Make-up by Katie Reynolds, ISBN 978-1-86205-918-4
Style Me Vintage: Clothes by Naomi Thompson, ISBN 978-1-86205-936-8
Style Me Vintage: Tea Parties by Betty Blythe, ISBN 978-1-86205-973-3
Style Me Vintage: Lookbook, ISBN 978-1-86205-976-4
Style Me Vintage: Accessories, ISBN 978-1-90981-500-1